GOOD KIDS

STRAIGHT TALK FROM
A PRODIGAL WHO CAME HOME

GONE BAD

JOSEPH F. MAXIM

WHITAKER
HOUSE

Unless otherwise indicated, all Scripture quotations are taken from the *The Holy Bible, English Standard Version*, © 2016, 2001, 2000, 1995 by Crossway Bibles, a division of Good News Publishers. Used by permission. All rights reserved. Scripture quotations marked (KJV) are taken from the King James Version of the Holy Bible.

Boldface type in the Scripture quotations indicates the author's emphasis.

GOOD KIDS GONE BAD
Straight Talk from a Prodigal Who Came Home

joseph.maxim7@gmail.com

ISBN: 979-8-88769-132-9
eBook ISBN: 979-8-88769-133-6
Printed in the United States of America
© 2024 by Joseph F. Maxim

Whitaker House
1030 Hunt Valley Circle
New Kensington, PA 15068
www.whitakerhouse.com

Library of Congress Control Number: 2024901222

1 2 3 4 5 6 7 8 9 10 11 Ⓦ 31 30 29 28 27 26 25 24

DEDICATION

I am dedicating this book to my mom. "MOM" turned upside down is "WOW"—Woman of Wonder. Through my mom's countless hours of prayers that led to bloodstained knees, all eight of her children have come to know Christ as their Savior. Thanks, Isobel Maxim, for your selfless life and your personal relationship to your heavenly Father.

CONTENTS

FOREWORD

It is an honor for me to write this foreword for my brother Joe. I have watched him and his wife, Chris, minister to young people for over twenty-five years with tremendous results. As you will read in the pages ahead, a person may be clean but still not free from the monsters that haunt them, from whatever drugs of choice enslave them. Joe and Chris strive to help young men and women be not just "clean" but also "totally free."

Their passion to see young adults become free is relentless. It is one thing to talk about becoming free from a lifestyle of destruction and quite another to be in the arena fighting alongside those who are struggling with seemingly no hope of change. Joe and Chris actually come alongside young people in their struggles, those who just can't seem to get out of the massive holes they are in.

I am one of the seven siblings Joe refers to in this book, and, yes, I am one of the those who was held captive by the forces of darkness because of choices I had made. Watching Joe and Chris up close and personal as they've devoted their lives to helping young adults become totally free has been both beautiful and awe-inspiring.

In the pages ahead Joe shares real-life tools that have proven effective in breaking the destructive habits of those struggling to be free from addictions. This book will not only give you tremendous insight into the fierce battle being waged in the souls of many young adults, but it will also impart truths so that you can be more effective in helping your loved one actually walk in total freedom for the rest of his or her life. The tools and truths you will discover in this little gem will better equip you to help your loved one while renewing hope in your heart to continue in the fight for his or her freedom and happiness.

When I think of a word to describe the work Joe and Chris do with young adults, it's the same word that describes the wisdom contained in this book: *authentic*. Read this book and be strengthened. Read this book and become wiser. Read this book and allow the hope you are seeking to take deep root in your heart.

—Jim Maxim

INTRODUCTION

The sound of my dad's car door woke me from dozing. I was mad at myself because I hadn't meant to fall asleep. The night before had not been good, and when Dad didn't come home from work right away, I knew he was at the bar again. At eleven years old, I already knew the six-foot four-inch, 285-pound man who was my father was an alcoholic. I would listen for his car and then scurry to find a place to hide. On a typical night like this one, he would come find me and pull me out from under the bed or wherever I was hiding. The amount of alcohol he had consumed would determine the kind of drunk I would face—the mean one or the nice one.

The nice one would pull me out, set me on his lap, and tell me how much he loved me. The mean one was abusive, and I'd know the size of my face by the size of his hand. Both the nice one and the mean one carried the sickening stink of the bar—stale cigarettes, beer, greasy food. I hated those smells and still find them hard to get out of my nostrils. The nice drunk dad, however, would bring home food: fish sandwiches, hot sausages…the bar smell was gross, but the bar food was heavenly.

I played football on Saturdays at my little Catholic school, and my dad usually served as the announcer. He was big, boisterous, and fun—everyone loved him—but I would be down on

11

the field, ashamed. I was already insecure about playing football, because back then I was small for my age; on top of that, I would be ashamed hearing my dad on the low-quality public address system, because I could tell he was drunk.

I still consider my home during my growing-up years to have been a loving, caring home, but because of my dad, it was highly dysfunctional. I am the youngest of eight kids—five boys and three girls. All five boys and one of the girls are alcoholics, and some are drug addicts. That's six of eight who are addicted to substances, six of eight who inherited this curse from my father. He died when I was just sixteen, from lung cancer and a brain tumor, but his legacy was already firmly in place.

DID OUR STRUGGLES WITH SUBSTANCE ABUSE
MEAN THAT WE WERE BAD KIDS? NO. WE
WERE NOT INHERENTLY WORSE THAN ANY
OTHER SINNER—WHICH IS EVERY HUMAN—BUT
OUR LIVES WERE PREDICTABLE GIVEN OUR
UPBRINGING. WE WERE, YOU MIGHT SAY, GOOD
KIDS GONE BAD.

My oldest brother was a Vietnam vet and a severe alcoholic; he died after several years of struggling with addiction. I have another brother who flew through the windshield of his car from driving under the influence and got a face full of stitches. Thankfully he defied the doctor's prediction that he wouldn't survive, and he has. Another brother had an alcohol-induced heart attack, and another has lived ten years past the eight days his doctor predicted because of liver disease and jaundice. One of my sisters struggles to get off pain pills, alcohol, and drugs of the benzodiazepine variety, such as Ativan, Klonopin, and Xanax. We are a mess, and every bit of it is predictable. Did our struggles with substance abuse mean that we were bad kids? No. We were not inherently worse than any other sinner—which is every human—but our lives were predictable given our upbringing. We were, you might say, good kids gone bad.

NATURE AND NURTURE

When a child is born, he or she is mostly a blank slate. God has certainly wired them to a small degree, but most of the wiring is done by parents, by caretakers, and by the environment. If you aren't sure about this, consider the following statistics.

According to the American Academy of Child & Adolescent Psychiatry, children of alcoholics are four times more likely to develop alcoholism than those who are not raised by alcoholics.[1] This increased risk is due to two main reasons: namely, genetics and environment.[2] Increasingly there is thought to be a genetic component to alcoholism. Additionally, when children are exposed to a lifestyle of alcoholism, it becomes normative for them. I have personally seen these patterns for alcoholism hold true for substance abuse in general, no matter the type of substance.

Neither of these two reasons—genetics or environment—has anything to do with the "badness" of the child. Good kids may have genetic predispositions to alcoholism, and good kids may be raised in environments where alcoholism is normative. These kids, in an important way, are victims of their circumstances.

Now please understand what I am *not* saying. I am not saying these kids are powerless or that their environments will automatically dictate the outcomes of their lives. A key factor in recovery

---

1. American Academy of Child & Adolescent Psychiatry, "Alcohol Use in Families," American Academy of Child & Adolescent Psychiatry, https://www.aacap.org/AACAP/Families_and_Youth/Facts_for_Families/FFF-Guide/Children-Of-Alcoholics-017 (accessed December 12, 2023).
2. National Institute on Alcohol Abuse and Alcoholism, "Genetics of Alcohol Use Disorder," National Institute of Health, https://www.niaaa.nih.gov/alcohols-effects-health/alcohol-use-disorder/genetics-alcohol-use-disorder (accessed December 12, 2023).

is taking responsibility for one's life and not giving in to deterministic victimhood. At the same time, it is crucial for those of us who care about these kids and want to help them to start with an understanding of the obstacles they face, including genetics and mindsets that have been trained by their environments.

Who among us is not impacted by the environment in which we are raised? Look at virtually any aspect of life, and you will observe clues about the way a person was brought up. Consider the way you think about money, marriage, and relationships. I guarantee your mindset was impacted by the way those closest to you handled money, marriage, and relationships. Thank Mom, Dad, family, and friends for these influences. You either adopted their thinking or you purposely rejected it and set out to do the exact opposite—sometimes successfully and sometimes not.

Since you're reading this book, I'll assume you have some kind of connection to alcoholism or substance abuse. Maybe you know and love someone you are desperate to help, perhaps one of your own children. Maybe you recognize some of your own mistakes and want to correct some of the damage you perceive to have done. Good for you! I'm proud of you for caring, for owning it, and for seeking ways to help. Maybe it's *you* who's trying to change, to gain freedom from the bondage of substance abuse. If you're the one who is in bondage, I'm proud of you for trying to change.

WHAT ABOUT THOSE NOT RAISED BY SUBSTANCE ABUSERS?

Before we go much further, I want to point out that although the child raised by substance abusers is more likely to struggle with addictions in adulthood than the child who is not raised by substance abusers, it is still the case that some kids fall into these addictions even when none of their caretakers is a substance abuser. They "go bad." But in this very fact lies our hope!

You might think that everything is determined. In some ways this is true—but only partially. If some kids who are raised by alcoholics do *not* become alcoholics, there must be a reason. Likewise, if some kids who are *not* raised by alcoholics *do* become alcoholics, there must also be a reason. But what is it? At the end of the day, God has given men and women, His image-bearers, free will. That means that although it might seem difficult, we can make choices. We can change.

AT THE END OF THE DAY,
GOD HAS GIVEN MEN AND WOMEN, HIS IMAGE-
BEARERS, FREE WILL. THAT MEANS THAT
ALTHOUGH IT MIGHT SEEM DIFFICULT, WE CAN
MAKE CHOICES. WE CAN CHANGE.

This is great news! Change is possible! You do not have to live in bondage forever. There is a God who cares about you and who has made a way for you to come to Him for freedom and for healing. There are concrete steps you can take—concrete steps I have seen work time and again in helping real people rise up from utter hopelessness and into new life. The reason I have written this book and have labored in my recovery ministry for so long is because I have seen what can happen when someone cares. When a person struggling with addictions finally makes the decision to try his or her best, change can happen. You can do this. Your loved ones can do this. Because God can do this!

In this book I will be as vulnerable as I can in hopes that it will help you. I'll share stories from my own journey and from the journeys of other "good kids gone bad." I want to not only fill you with hope but also give you a road map of God's way for getting and staying free.

STARTING YOUNG: MY OWN JOURNEY INTO ADDICTION

I started drinking as a boy. At a young age I would steal beers from my dad, and he didn't have enough wherewithal to even notice. By age thirteen, I was smoking marijuana. I'll never forget that first time—where I was and what it felt like. An older guy got me high, and I remember that I was nervous and that my body loved it. My journey into addiction started right then and there.

As I said earlier, I was a small kid. I was also awkward, backward, and barely able to string a sentence together under any sort of social pressure. I had a severe confidence problem, and to compensate, I felt drawn to muscles. I felt that if I got big enough and strong enough, I could change my life, so I went for it—and I was all in. I was as addicted to working out as I was to anything else. The hunger to get big merged with my propensity to use substances, and I began taking steroids in high school. I drank, I smoked weed, I juiced, I lifted weights, and I got bigger, and bigger, and bigger.

I actually became a good enough volleyball player in high school to have a shot at college scholarships, but my obsession was bodybuilding, so I blew off a couple of offers. My plan was to become a professional bodybuilder. This turned out to be a disaster for me, because every time I got into bodybuilding, I took steroids, which would lead to my taking other addictive drugs and alcohol. So, although I was getting big and strong, I never really looked good enough to compete because of all the other stuff.

In time my body got too accustomed to the marijuana for it to do anything for me. That was when I started doing cocaine. I loved frying it up and smoking it. Addiction had fully taken me over. I was getting high every day that I could while continuing to get huge from lifting weights and taking steroids.

ADDICTION HAD FULLY TAKEN ME OVER. I WAS GETTING HIGH EVERY DAY THAT I COULD WHILE CONTINUING TO GET HUGE FROM LIFTING WEIGHTS AND TAKING STEROIDS.

I lived like this for some time until one Friday afternoon in December 1987. I worked six to seven days a week as a bricklayer, and although I spent a lot of money on drinking and drugs, I always had a dollar in my pocket to go out on the weekends with my "get high" buddies. On this particular Friday I was going to finish my workout, get cleaned up, and go party—the usual. As I wrapped up my workout at the gym that day, I noticed a poster on the wall that read, "Come see the cutting-edge ministry of Dan Judge and his wife." There was a picture of them both, looking ripped and powerful.

The poster intrigued me, but I certainly was not planning to attend. What I planned to do was get high and party. After my workout I took that week's paycheck and went and bought myself some new clothes and gold jewelry, along with a couple of eight balls—cocaine wrapped up in pieces of paper—and got ready to hit the clubs. I called my buddies but couldn't get any of them on the phone. (It was 1987, which meant no cell phones.)

All dressed up with nowhere to go, sitting in my little Toyota truck, I started thinking about that poster with the ripped couple on it. Next thing I knew, I was sitting in the last row, third seat, of a Full Gospel Church, watching some guy break bats and handcuffs, rip phone books, and destroy rubber hot water bottles. After that, he shared about Jesus. His obvious method was to draw a crowd with feats of strength and then share the gospel.

When the show was over, I went up to meet him. He held out his hand to shake mine, but I pushed it away. "You're a hypocrite, a liar!" I said angrily. "You're a steroid freak! You *and* your wife! How can you tell anyone about this God thing while you're addicted to steroids?"

I don't remember how he responded. I think I probably had turned and left before he had a chance.

AN APPOINTMENT WITH GOD

The next day, December 12, 1987, was Saturday, and again, after work, I got some more cocaine and some more party clothes and prepared to go out and tie one on for the night. Once more, I couldn't find any of my partying friends, and I again found myself at that same church, last row, third seat in, surrounded by brown chairs and brown carpet in this gym-turned-sanctuary.

As I sat there listening to Dan Judge talk about the power of God in Jesus Christ, I suddenly started to sweat. My stomach churned, and my heart pumped furiously as if I were having a heart attack. I thought all the cocaine in me was reacting with the alcohol and the steroids, and I genuinely thought for a minute that I was about to die. All the drugs weren't mixing well, I thought, and my heart just couldn't take it. I gripped the seat in front of me as I felt myself about to go down.

At that moment, I heard Judge saying, "Behold, I stand at the door and knock. If anyone hears my voice and opens the door, I will come in and dine with you and you with me." (See Revelation 3:20.)

As I was crashing, I thought, "What the heck does that mean?" Suddenly, in the midst of it all, I felt a tap on my shoulder, but when I turned to see who it was, *there was no one there.*

Before I knew it, I was standing up, leaving my row, and walking down the aisle to the front. There may as well have been no one else in that room, because I had tunnel vision, completely focused on reaching that spot at the altar. In my peripheral vision I could see my boys from the gym, there on my left, and I saw my coke buddies, there on my right, but I turned back to my target and just kept on moving—or, I should say, I kept on being moved. I arrived at the front and heard myself saying, "Dear Jesus, please come into my life. Forgive me my sins, and from this day forward help me to live for You."

There was no great revelation, no lights or fireworks that went off. There may have been a party in heaven, but on earth, all was quiet. I just finished praying, turned and left the building, and got into my little Toyota truck. But as I drove to my girl-friend's house, I knew something was different, and as I drove, I began tossing cocaine packets out the window. I think I tossed seven or eight of them, but I did decide to keep one of them, thinking, "Just in case this God thing isn't real, I'll have at least one as backup."

THERE WAS NO GREAT REVELATION, NO LIGHTS OR FIREWORKS THAT WENT OFF. THERE MAY HAVE BEEN A PARTY IN HEAVEN, BUT ON EARTH, ALL WAS QUIET.

I stopped at my girlfriend's and told her about what had happened, and then I went home to my mom. I remember pulling into the driveway and seeing her through the kitchen window of her small ranch house. She was bent over the sink doing the dishes, a woman of sorrows, a widow with a lot of kids, nearly all of whom were worrying her to death. She was crying as I came in.

"You forgot these," she said, sliding something across the counter. I looked down and saw two loaded syringes. This was nothing new for my mom, but she had found them in my room recently and was clearly at her wit's end.

"Mom," I said, "I met someone tonight."

"I know," she responded. "You met Dan Judge."

I had already told her about attending that first meeting, and she must have assumed I had gone back. I don't remember if her voice had any trace of hope in it, and I honestly don't know why it would have. She was acquainted with grief and not accustomed to getting good news from her family.

I persisted. "No, mom," I said. "I met *Somebody*."

Somehow, she discerned my meaning and realized there had been a change in me. Her tears of sorrow transformed into tears of hope, and her little Pentecostal hands rose in the air in gratitude to the One who had answered her most fervent prayers.

"Oh, Father, thank You!" she cried. She put her hands back down on the counter to support herself and said it again: "Oh, Father, thank You!"

Have you ever seen the culmination of years' worth of hard, gut-wrenching work? Have you ever struggled to bear fruit, feeling almost hopeless and powerless, only to finally see a ray of light, some sign that your work, your prayers, your passion, and your worry were not in vain? That was what I witnessed that day in that dear woman in front of me.

"I don't think I'm going to need these anymore," I assured her as I picked up the syringes and got ready to throw them away. I knew something in my life was dramatically different.

A NEW DAY

When I woke up the next day, my mom had a Bible for me called *The Living Word*. Inside the front cover she had written, "December 12, 1987. Today I met Jesus." That started a new journey in life for me, not only in sobriety but also in the true freedom that is found only in Christ. As I will say again and again in this book, there is a huge difference between being clean and being free—but on that special day, I was both.

THERE IS A HUGE DIFFERENCE BETWEEN
BEING CLEAN AND BEING FREE—
BUT ON THAT SPECIAL DAY, I WAS BOTH.

It was a new day, the start of a new era, but I wasn't quite sure what to do next. If I had been thinking clearly, I would have made a to-do list: "Number 1: Lose most of my friends. Number 2: Get to church. Number 3: Go to AA. Number 4: Start helping with youth group at Mom's church." I wanted to do whatever it would take to keep me on the right path, and it turns out that these were the next steps to help me do just that.

When I first started helping at youth group, the pastor asked me to give my testimony. This shook me. The whole reason I had worked out so much and taken drugs was because I had low self-esteem and could barely talk to people. Drugs and muscles got me into a lot of trouble—but they also made me feel more confident. I was terrified of public speaking, but somehow, I got through it.

The leader told me I should come early for a prayer meeting on Wednesday nights before youth group each week. I told him I would try but would miss some nights because of the USVBA (United States Volleyball Association) team I was going to be on.

"Okay," he said, "but next week you are going to have to decide. Either you fully commit to the Lord Jesus, or you fully commit to yourself."

THE MAP OF MY LIFE

I was a little taken aback by this line he had drawn in the sand. "Who does he think he is?" I thought to myself. But the next week, I was there for the prayer meeting. The leader gave me a little card with a prayer request on it: "Please help Johnny in school." In this way I began learning how to pray, both corporately and alone.

Eventually that youth pastor left, and the Lord brought us a new youth pastor. One week prior to the new youth pastor's arrival, we had a guest speaker. In prayer before the meeting, the guest speaker stopped prayer and said, "When you do what God is telling you to do, they will come like the wind." He stopped and said it again for a second time. The third time he said it, he slammed his hand on the table, picked up a napkin, and wrote on it "Psalm 82:3–5." He then looked me in the eyes and said, "When you do what God is telling you to do, they are going to come like a slow and steady wind."

This passage in Psalms reads:

> *"Give justice to the weak and the fatherless; maintain the right of the afflicted and the destitute. Rescue the weak and the needy; deliver them from the hand of the wicked." They have neither knowledge nor understanding, they walk about in darkness; all the foundations of the earth are shaken.*
>
> (Psalm 82:3–5 ESV)

Next to this verse in the margins of my Bible, I wrote, "10/1/95. Thank You, Jesus, for Your Word. Please show me how."

I became the right-hand man of the new youth pastor and did anything that needed to be done. I started teaching and sharing a little, and then one day, as I was sitting at my dining room table, I said, "Lord, what do I do with my life?"

"I want you to start a ten-step program," He said, "one that helps young people who are battling addiction." I knew this was a Holy Spirit moment. I wrote "YOU" at the top of the page— Young Overcomers United. I realized that the Lord was speaking to me.

The concept and the responsibility that came with it scared me, so I closed the book. I continued working with the youth group for the next few weeks, and then we got another youth pastor. I took a risk and told him what I thought the Lord had said. He literally laughed in my face. I don't know whether I was offended or relieved, but I decided to just drop it and forget about it.

"He's been walking with the Lord a lot longer than I have," I thought, "so he must know. I'm just a dreamer, and I'm nothing. I didn't really hear from the Lord."

This thing tormented me, though. I just couldn't shake the thought.

At that point in time I didn't know a thing about how to start a nonprofit. I thought you had to do all kinds of stuff like make T-shirts and hats, get a building, hire staff, and endure all kinds of headaches. The reality, however, is that the nonprofit the Lord had called me to establish began with just one young man in our home—and within eighteen months, it had grown to more than twenty people.

They came every Thursday, and my wife would cook for them. (By this point I was married, and we had two kids.) The young people who came especially enjoyed the homemade food. I remember one young man saying it was "the bomb." The ball was rolling, and people started to notice. The magistrates in our area caught wind of what we were doing, and newspapers started publishing articles about us. This was all crazy to us because we had only just signed the papers establishing our nonprofit status, but it must have seemed like we knew what we were doing.

One of the neatest things I witnessed during this time was that as people entered our home, they would leave their "tough guy" act at the door. They dropped their façades and bared their hearts, and when they opened up to us, it was incredible. Their transparency let us know we were on the right path.

AS PEOPLE ENTERED OUR HOME,
THEY WOULD LEAVE THEIR "TOUGH GUY" ACT AT
THE DOOR. THEY DROPPED THEIR FAÇADES
AND BARED THEIR HEARTS, AND WHEN THEY
OPENED UP TO US, IT WAS INCREDIBLE.

As I love to say, there's a huge difference between being clean and being free. Our goal was to promote freedom, and if you're going to help someone become free, you really have to get to know them. Just as no two fingerprints are alike, so no two people are alike. Each person's life has its own unique "fingerprint," so to speak. If you're going to help people, you have to get to know their fingerprints, the way they move through the world, their home life, and why they think the way they think. You have to know what makes them who they are. We were glad these people felt comfortable being themselves in our home because it meant we might have a chance to help them.

I never looked down on the people who came in each Thursday. You never know what someone is going through until you get to know them a little. In our ministry, we live by the "1,440 principle," which says that since we have only 1,440 minutes each day, we had better be intentional about how we spend them. How many minutes were we willing to give someone to help them become a better person, knowing that we would never get those minutes back? People would come into our house every Thursday and stay late, sometimes as late as two in the morning. Keep in mind, I am a bricklayer; I had to get up at a quarter past four to go to work. As long as we were helping these people, though, I wasn't going to make them leave. I was more than willing to invest those minutes in helping them.

HELL ATTACKS

Fast-forward a few years, and my kids were getting older. The heartbeat of our ministry was strong. The phone rang twenty-four hours a day, seven days a week, and we were doing everything on a volunteer basis. I tried to raise money for the ministry, because I was committed, but I also had mouths to feed, and it became harder and harder to keep it up while working full-time.

My son was sixteen years old, and my daughter was fresh out of high school. We drove her to college for her first year, and before we left, I told her one of the stupidest things I've ever said in my life: "Look behind me, sweetheart. You're off of my shirttails. If you want to run with the devil, you're going to live like hell." Before the semester was over, she came home and told us she was pregnant. Apparently, she had taken my words as a suggestion, not a warning. I'll never stop regretting those words.

PROUD PAPA MOMENT

Prior to my daughter's news, my son was in a car accident in which he sustained almost fatal injuries. His lungs collapsed, and he had bleeding in his brain. He was on the edge of life and death, and we were convinced he wasn't going to make it, but his story is incredible.

He had been at a sweet sixteen party where there was alcohol, something we didn't know about until later, and he did something we never thought he would do: He got into a car with someone who was drunk. They flew over an embankment close to our house, and a tree collapsed on top of the car. He was not breathing, and they transferred him by helicopter to the emergency room at Allegheny General Hospital in Pittsburgh, a major trauma unit.

I got there as quickly as I could. This is when I first used what I now call *faith words*. When I saw him, I said, "That's not my son." He was lying there hooked up to a breathing machine and with these contraptions on his legs, and they were getting ready to put a shunt in his head to try to reduce the swelling. That's when the Lord allowed these words to come to me in a proud papa moment: "Hell, is this all you got? You're going to try to take my son's life with a little bit of high and drink? He is going to talk again, going to walk again, and going to fish again. Take the pictures now, because this will be his testimony."

JOURNEY

It's been a long journey, and we're still in it. My son has a traumatic brain injury (TBI). We are those people who seem to always experience trials and tribulations. Every time we try to take a step in the right direction, hell comes and beats us up—or at least tries to. My son's injury and my daughter's pregnancy, however, turned out to be two of the biggest blessings of my life.

Our testimony is that even when trials come for our kids, they can turn it around to do incredible things. My son is now twenty-seven and works as a fly-fishing guide out West. Before his accident, my son had a 4.0 GPA and was a three-sport athlete looking to go to Westpoint. After the accident, the doctor said he could never do anything again that requires a helmet. Although living with the TBI has been difficult, my son is a true overcomer, and the Lord has incredible plans to use him.

My daughter's son, an incredible blessing to our family, is now ten years old, and I am a happy grandpa. My daughter is an awesome mom, and my grandson is as smart as can be. We are in our twenty-seventh year of ministry to the young, hurting, broken hearts of the addicted, and Satan has not been able to stop us yet; we just keep plugging away.

Most people think an addict is someone who doesn't work and is dirty all the time, but nothing could be further from the truth. The road to addiction always starts somewhere, and we try to find out just where a person is on that road, how far into the addiction cycle they are. Then we come alongside them and plant seeds of hope, water them, and then see the fruit. God has been so good to us. Right before the COVID pandemic we had done thirty-eight interventions in one year. I hope I never have to do that again, because it was a lot, each one lasting three hours. But it is good, grueling work that the Lord uses to produce good fruit.

THE ROAD TO ADDICTION ALWAYS STARTS SOMEWHERE, AND WE TRY TO FIND OUT JUST WHERE A PERSON IS ON THAT ROAD, HOW FAR INTO THE ADDICTION CYCLE THEY ARE.

We have learned so much through our own family's journey and through helping these young people. Our society's normalization of drugs and alcohol has created a vicious cycle for those who are addicted. We know that sharing our testimony puts us in arm's reach of these kids. We have lots of opportunities to communicate and to share what we have learned about the process of addiction, about how a young person can go so bad so quickly. Fundamentally we are all selfish and want pleasure, and this can spiral into an addiction.

HOW GOOD KIDS GO BAD

You see, when we talk about good kids going bad, it's important to realize it's not just kids coming from rough families with parents who do drugs. Some come from broken homes, but some come from great families. Some come from not-so-good parents, and others come from the supposed greatest parents in the world. No matter who the addicted person, and no matter what kind of background that person comes from, he or she just made one bad choice, and the path to addiction began there. Nobody wants to start down the slippery slope, but that's what happens.

NOBODY WANTS TO START DOWN THE SLIPPERY SLOPE, BUT THAT'S WHAT HAPPENS.

I have been to twenty funerals in twenty-seven years because one bad choice led to two bad choices, which led to ten. It's gut-wrenching. We recently lost three young men in the span of five months. They all loved the Lord, but they had freedom to choose, and they chose to use again.

GRACE AND FREEDOM

God is good and offers saving grace and the chance to walk in freedom. When you walk in freedom, you know who you are in Christ, and you know that your name is written in the Lamb's Book of Life. We promote freedom in our ministry, and we understand that we must give grace, upon grace, upon grace—and when we're done giving grace, we must give even more, because this path to freedom requires abundant grace.

Only the person struggling with addiction knows just how bad it really is, and we need to be gracious with him or her. The road to recovery is different for everyone, so we personalize it for each person. We meet as a group every Thursday night, and the hardest part is teaching these kids how to live again. My wife mentors the women, and I work with the men. Our mission statement is simple but powerful: To create a pathway enabling young addicts to take steps to freedom. God wants to set the captives free!

What follows is a series of frameworks to help navigate that path to freedom. Each framework is an attempt to solve the same problem: the perceived lack of freedom that led to the bondage of substance abuse in the first place and the process of regaining that freedom. Some chapters will no doubt resonate with you, while others may not; but if you read them all, your understanding will be transformed about how "good kids go bad" and about how this change can be reversed. When we relentlessly renew our minds with truths about who we are in Christ, true transformation can occur.

WE PROMOTE FREEDOM IN OUR MINISTRY,
AND WE UNDERSTAND THAT WE MUST GIVE
GRACE, UPON GRACE, UPON GRACE—AND WHEN
WE'RE DONE GIVING GRACE, WE MUST GIVE
EVEN MORE, BECAUSE THIS PATH TO FREEDOM
REQUIRES ABUNDANT GRACE.

TWO PARTS

This book comes from my years of speaking on the topic of addiction and recovery, and each chapter was born out of material that was first given as a talk. Some chapters deal with *preventing* good kids from going bad; the contents show parents and caregivers what kinds of things can be done at home to ensure the best possible outcomes for the kids they are raising. The other chapters deal with recovery; they outline how to help someone who has already gotten into trouble with alcohol and drugs. Part One will cover prevention, and Part Two will deal with recovery.

I wish I didn't know so much about this topic, but it is my hope and prayer to put this hard-won wisdom to work in your service and in the service of all the "good kids" we know and love.

PART ONE:
AN OUNCE OF PREVENTION

Can substance abuse be prevented? I believe it can. I only wish I had known what I know now a long time ago. In Part One I share my best understanding of how to prevent the downward spiral that can plummet good kids into bad addictions. Having witnessed hundreds of addictions and having walked with many recovering addicts, I believe there are clear warning signs to addiction and helpful actionable steps that can be taken long before recovery is necessary.

If you are in a situation where you are already beyond prevention, read this anyway, because what is helpful for prevention is also helpful for understanding addiction in general and for helping with recovery.

ONE

THE CULTIVATING STAGE

Have you ever grown a garden or cared for a lawn? When you grow things—whether it's produce, flowers, or any sort of plant—you *cultivate* them. Humanity has learned to do this over the generations, including how to find good soil for planting our seeds. We know the difference between good soil, sandy soil, and rocky soil.

Jesus made an analogy between soil and spiritual growth. (See Matthew 13:3–9, 18–23.) He said some seed falls on good ground, some on not-so-good ground, and some on bad ground. One thing is consistent, however: The seed always falls somewhere.

ALWAYS BEING CULTIVATED

We must understand that our kids are being cultivated every day, whether by us or by someone else. Every day they are growing and changing physically, but they are also growing and changing *spiritually*. If we are not cultivating their growth, someone or something else is. We know from God's Word that the thief comes to rob, to kill, and to destroy. We also know that Jesus came to give life and to give it abundantly. (See John 10:10.) Will our children grow in rocky, shallow soil, influenced by the thief? Or will they grow in the fertile soil of abundant and eternal life, influenced by God through us?

WILL OUR CHILDREN GROW IN ROCKY,
SHALLOW SOIL, INFLUENCED BY THE THIEF?
OR WILL THEY GROW IN THE FERTILE SOIL
OF ABUNDANT AND ETERNAL LIFE,
INFLUENCED BY GOD THROUGH US?

Spiritually speaking, the abundant life is a surrendered life, and this must be cultivated. Most young people see blessings as things that are just super positive in their lives, such as gifts, money, or acts of kindness. Blessings come in many forms, however, and the cultivating stage of the abundant life—even though it is hard, hard work—is a blessing. It's difficult for children to understand that hard work can be a blessing, but it is an important lesson to learn.

Consider the farmer. When he rises early in the morning, he cultivates, which is nothing but hard work. There is even a good chance that, because of weather or some farming mistake, nothing will grow at all, but a good farmer will continue to cultivate. He will learn, he will understand, he will adjust, and he will do whatever it takes to grow a crop. This concept of cultivating applies to many areas of life, and our eyes must be open to the fact that there is a cultivating stage of spiritual growth that lasts a lifetime. Our sanctification is a lifelong process whereby God grows us into the likeness of His Son. It's a lot of work for God and for us.

CULTIVATING, PRUNING, AND RESTING

During sanctification we need to understand which things need to be *cultivated* and which things need to be *pruned*. The Bible talks a lot about inheritances. As humans we have inherited a sin nature, and it is this nature, along with the following such manifestations of it, that we are called to prune during our sanctification process:

Now the works of the flesh are evident: sexual immorality, impurity, sensuality, idolatry, sorcery, enmity, strife, jealousy, fits of anger, rivalries, dissensions, divisions, envy, drunkenness, orgies, and things like these. I warn you, as I warned you before, that those who do such things will not inherit the kingdom of God. (Galatians 5:19–21)

Those who have trusted in Jesus, however, also have a new nature, a nature that we've inherited from the Lord, and these are the types of things we are called to cultivate:

But the fruit of the Spirit is love, joy, peace, patience, kindness, goodness, faithfulness, gentleness, self-control; against such things there is no law. And those who belong to Christ Jesus have crucified the flesh with its passions and desires. (Galatians 5:22–24)

Every good farmer knows that an important part of cultivating is allowing the land to rest. He will leave a portion of his farm or garden dormant every few years so that nutrients in the soil can be replenished. This practice has profound parallels to the life of a young person. There are seasons when it is okay, even good, for young people to sit and do nothing, to relax. It is wise for them to just sit and be washed in the water of the Word (see Ephesians 5:26), to hear gospel truths from family, church members, and parents—Mom and especially Dad.

THERE ARE SEASONS WHEN IT IS OKAY,
EVEN GOOD, FOR YOUNG PEOPLE TO SIT AND DO
NOTHING, TO RELAX. IT IS WISE FOR THEM
TO JUST SIT AND BE WASHED IN
THE WATER OF THE WORD.

I often say that the fatherless heart will not produce, but the reality is that it will produce *something*—just not something that we probably want. When we look for the reasons why good kids go bad, we must consider what has been cultivated in their lives. Can you put an orange tree in a cornfield and expect it to grow corn? You cannot. Neither can you plant corn seeds in an orange grove and expect them to produce oranges. When we cultivate hearts, the same principles are at play. We must cultivate specific things in the lives of the young people under our influence so that they can stay strong and produce the sort of fruit God designed for them to bear.

Many people are familiar with the expression "You inherit everything from your fathers and forefathers." Usually we are referring to sin principles with this saying; we inherit the *sins* of our fathers. This is no doubt true, but the principle applies to what is positive, as well. Our children also inherit what is good about their fathers and forefathers, and we can help encourage these good things by more actively cultivating those positive traits in them.

CULTIVATE WHAT THEY ARE

Just as infertile soil will not produce a crop, so too will a person struggle to produce good things if we place them in an area where they cannot grow. In fact, when we do this, we hurt them. We misunderstand their gifts, their talents, and their personalities, and we try to cultivate something that they are not.

Have you ever seen parents get overly involved in their child's sport activities, even though the child does not have an athletic bone in his or her body? Or perhaps you have seen a parent push a musical instrument on a kid who hates it and has no aptitude for it. To cultivate a child's gifts, we must really know the child and his or her unique giftings. If we, as parents, truly believe God's Word that we are "*fearfully and wonderfully made*" (Psalm 139:14), then we must accept that this cultivating stage depends on our understanding that the plan for each kid is *specific*.

TO CULTIVATE A CHILD'S GIFTS, WE MUST REALLY KNOW THE CHILD AND HIS OR HER UNIQUE GIFTINGS.

Some kids are not meant to be public speakers. Some are not meant to be athletes. Some are not meant to be singers, dancers, songwriters, mathematicians, engineers, teachers, or whatever other career path we may have chosen for them. There is nothing wrong with your children in this regard. God made them how He made them. He has given them some gifts and talents, and He has withheld others. This applies to 100 percent of the human population. What matters is discerning what God has given a person to do—His calling on their life.

There is one thing we do know for sure about calling: God has called each person to be a child of the living God. Too often, however, we allow this to become pie-in-the-sky faith that doesn't actually impact our day-to-day living. We forget that life comes along and smacks our kids in the face with certain situations and challenges, such as drugs and alcohol. On the way to understand themselves as God's children, young people must wade through the chaos of sin and darkness in this fallen world, trying to figure out the meaning of life, who God is, who they are, and why they are here. The more we can help them through that process, the better. The more guidance we can give along the way, the less likely they will be to give up and try to "escape" through substance abuse.

This cultivating stage must be accepted. Again, if you consider the farmer, out on a tractor cultivating his field, common sense will tell you what he's doing: He is digging up the field for new growth, preparing the soil to receive the seeds that he will plant, so that the plants will thrive in that field. The farmer *expects* growth.

He wants it, and he knows from experience, trials, and knowledge that he must first cultivate that field in order to grow the crop he expects. Parents must operate the same way—we need to *expect* growth, and we need to *accept* that cultivating is essential to getting there.

AS PARENTS, WE NEED TO *EXPECT* GROWTH, AND WE NEED TO *ACCEPT* THAT CULTIVATING IS ESSENTIAL TO GETTING THERE.

If your kids perform off the charts at school and understand math easily, cultivate that aptitude; but if they struggle with school and you find that they learn differently, don't think poorly of them. They are not "bad people." Some people learn visually, some audibly, others more kinesthetically, and some have trouble learning in any of the conventional ways. Anyone can be successful in life. Just because a person may not have natural book smarts does not mean he is incapable of learning. People just need to be cultivated in the right way.

Some kids are good at sports. Putting your kids on sports teams cultivates their athletic ability, sense of teamwork, friendships, sportsmanship, work ethic, and more. Tryouts are often used as tools to differentiate between various skill levels, and kids might be assigned to different teams—A team, B team, in-house team, travel team, and so on. Many parents think their kids are the best and should go straight to the top, but we must teach our kids as we go. We must slowly cultivate these skills along the way and teach them to play with heart.

SEASONS

Cultivation is an ongoing process on every farm and in every garden. After the plants grow and are harvested, the process starts all over. The soil must be churned up, fertilized again, and then replanted for next year's harvest. The same holds true for our children. Cultivation never stops.

One specific area we can cultivate that will yield lifelong benefits is how our children handle mistakes. When children mess up, those are great opportunities to accept their mistakes, talk about them, and help them understand what happened. We can teach them in these moments, and hopefully they will learn. It might take their making the same mistake two, three, or four times before they learn the lesson. So be it. Cultivation is still happening.

Sometimes when a farmer is cultivating, the tractor breaks, he runs out of gas, or it starts raining. It seems that everything is conspiring against successful cultivation. By analogy, consider the single parent who works all day, keeps house all night, and still must try to find time to cultivate a child—it's hard to do after you've already given everything you have! Here are where godly support networks are essential. Single parents need God's people to come alongside them and help them in the daunting task of cultivating their children.

In the offseason the farmer will take care of his equipment so that it is working at 100 percent capacity when the next season begins. When farmers maintain their equipment, they are preparing to cultivate. They understand the purpose of each season, including the offseason. In the cultivating season they aren't looking at their watches; they're looking at the sun because from sunup to sundown is cultivating time. And they don't need calendars to make schedules because the seasons dictate their schedule. They know what is going to happen in winter, spring, summer, and fall. This concept of seasons can help us understand the life of a child. As God reminds us in His Word, there is a season for everything:

For everything there is a season, and a time for every matter under heaven: a time to be born, and a time to die; a time to plant, and a time to pluck up what is planted.

(Ecclesiastes 3:1–2)

Sometimes we want to cultivate maturity or other character-istics in our kids when it is simply not yet time. Just as a farmer has many cultivating tasks—tilling the soil, sowing the seed, removing weeds, harvesting the produce—so too does cultivating a child take on many forms, but each is most appropriate at its proper time. Would you plow a field at harvesttime? Of course you wouldn't, because that's the season for harvesting. In the same way, whatever we cultivate must be cultivated according to the proper season.

JUST AS A FARMER HAS MANY CULTIVATING TASKS—TILLING THE SOIL, SOWING THE SEED, REMOVING WEEDS, HARVESTING THE PRODUCE— SO TOO DOES CULTIVATING A CHILD TAKE ON MANY FORMS, BUT EACH IS MOST APPROPRIATE AT ITS PROPER TIME.

An important question to ask when seeking to understand these cultivating stages is "Why?" *Why* did she start drinking? *Why* did he start having sex at such a young age? *Why* did she stop attending church? *Why* did he start doing drugs? Although this isn't always the case, the answer to these "why" questions is often, "Because no one else was doing the cultivating."

If we aren't intentionally cultivating the things of God in our children, then something else *will* step in and fill that cultivation void. Something seemingly more attractive than the God in you will come along to take on the job. Know this: All kids look up to their parents. If they don't have a parent present in the home— not just physically present but also spiritually, emotionally, intellectually—they will look for one. They long for someone or something to fill that void, and they will find it.

Even in depressed and downtrodden areas, kids will seek figures to follow. They want to be nurtured and cultivated. There is something innate in all of us that wants to grow. Will we rise to the challenge and intentionally help cultivate good things in our kids? Or will we thoughtlessly nurture bad habits and mindsets?

WILL WE RISE TO THE CHALLENGE AND INTENTIONALLY HELP CULTIVATE GOOD THINGS IN OUR KIDS? OR WILL WE THOUGHTLESSLY NURTURE BAD HABITS AND MINDSETS?

We can cultivate both good and bad in our kids. For instance, we can cultivate a mentality of being taken care of or one of self-reliance. If you cultivate a poor work ethic and an attitude that says, "Oh, well; you can't change things, you just have to accept them," you will see that when that child grows up, he won't get a job; he won't want to work. He will want to rely on you or someone else to take care of him. A mindset of helplessness has been cultivated. What a detriment to himself and to society.

TOOLS AND TASKS OF CULTIVATING

Words can cultivate. High fives can cultivate. Giving can cultivate. The fact is, we are cultivating every single day. Young people are spying on us adults and seeing our examples. They see the ways we interact with them and with each other. They see if we are encouraging them and building them up or discouraging them and tearing them down. We cultivate the way they think and even their personalities.

WORDS CAN CULTIVATE. HIGH FIVES CAN
CULTIVATE. GIVING CAN CULTIVATE. THE FACT
IS, WE ARE CULTIVATING EVERY SINGLE DAY.

There are many types of personalities, and each one must be cultivated. My daughter, who is my firstborn, turned out to be exactly like me. There is a saying that firstborns turn out like their dads, and I have seen that to be true. Whatever strength and zeal they use to approach life is often a direct result of Dad. Dads, your kids are watching and learning from you. What are you cultivating in their lives and hearts?

Even after you cultivate the soil and plant the seed, you still must water it. If a seed does not get watered, it will dry up and die. In the same way, if we do not continually nurture and care for young people with our loving words, actions, hugs, and well-timed affirmations to build confidence, then the good things we've planted will dry up and wither. When they face obstacles, they may turn away, saying, "It's too hard. I can't." Cultivation means carefully tending to what we have already planted so that there can be growth, no matter what. If a farmer has to run irrigation lines farther so that the seeds he planted won't dry up, he does it. We, too, must be willing to do whatever it takes to ensure the seeds we have planted are getting watered so that they do not dry up and die.

God's Word says, *"Train up a child in the way he should go; even when he is old he will not depart from it"* (Proverbs 22:6). It is possible for a child to climb onto the cultivation tractor and just ride along, never growing. Parents who struggled growing up sometimes want to make things easier for their own kids. They want to give, provide, and just make life better for their kids. If you grew up with nothing and worked hard to get where you are, it feels good to give your kids everything you never had growing up. When you do this, however, you cultivate the wrong kind of attitude—you cultivate laziness and a sense of entitlement.

Cultivating is easy. Cultivating *well* is hard. It is a lot of hard, grueling work, and it takes intentionality and constantly living out good, godly things for our kids to see and emulate. If you are trying to cultivate a spiritual prayer life in your kids, then your kids have to see you praying every day. They need to know that Mom, Dad, or whoever their guardian may be rises every single day to sit in the presence of God in prayer, preparing for the tasks of the day ahead. We lead by example. How we live our own lives is, in and of itself, *cultivation.*

CULTIVATING IS EASY. CULTIVATING *WELL*
IS HARD. IT IS A LOT OF HARD, GRUELING
WORK, AND IT TAKES INTENTIONALITY AND
CONSTANTLY LIVING OUT THE GOOD THINGS
FOR OUR KIDS TO SEE AND EMULATE.

When I die, I want my kids to be able to say, "My dad was in prayer every day." My wife understands nowadays that if she doesn't see coffee stains on my Bible or me sitting in my prayer place at the usual time, then something is wrong. To cultivate goodness in our kids, we have to take the responsibility of the farmer, the person given charge, and lead by example. The Bible says, *"Moreover, it is required of stewards that they be found faithful"* (1 Corinthians 4:2). We've been given this charge by God, and we must be found faithful in fulfilling it.

We all have different personalities and giftings, different levels of authority and ability—but we *all* have to sleep, eat, and apply these biblical principles in some way within the sphere where God has placed us. Some farmers work thousand-acre farms, others have three acres, and some just have small gardens in their back-yards; but each one must face the same responsibility. The dirt must be turned up, fertilizer spread, seeds planted and cultivated, weeds pulled. So, too, we all are called to cultivate, wherever God has placed us.

Cultivating is nothing but hard work at any level, and it may be that after cultivating for months and months, you still do not see any growth. But know this: God's Word will never come back void or empty. That is His promise! (See Isaiah 55:11.)

CULTIVATING GOD'S PROMISES

There are a lot of good things we are called to cultivate in our kids' lives, but the most important things we must cultivate within them are God's promises. Are we telling them the promises of God? The most important promise is that because Jesus died for us on the cross and rose again from the grave, there is a place for us in heaven with Him. When we die, we can walk those streets of gold.

Do your kids know this truth? Has this promise been cultivated in them? Never stop sowing and watering this profound promise, because it is the foundational promise on which all the others stand. Tell your kids about those streets of gold, those walls of jasper (see Revelation 21:11, 21). Teach them about the river of life flowing from the throne of God (see Revelation 22:1). Tell them about their Father's house in eternity where they can live with Him and His Son.

This is where our encouragement must come from—His Word, His promises. Don't raise your kids merely on "Do this" and "Don't do that." *Show them* what God's Word says. *Tell them* of the promise in the Word of God that they *"may have life and have it abundantly"* (John 10:10). Tell them what God says about walking by the Spirit—that if they do, they *"will not gratify the desires of the flesh"* (Galatians 5:16). Cultivate in them the promise that *"they who wait for the* Lord *shall renew their strength; they shall mount up with wings like eagles; they shall run and not be weary; they shall walk and not faint"* (Isaiah 40:31). Teach them what Romans 8:31 says: *"If God is for us, who can be against us?"* Nurture them with these truths. Cultivate their hearts with the promises of God in His Word. If we are not cultivating that, then what are we cultivating?

DON'T RAISE YOUR KIDS MERELY ON "DO THIS" AND "DON'T DO THAT." *SHOW THEM* WHAT GOD'S WORD SAYS.

Every year I am laid off seasonally from construction. During this season I spend extra time with my grandson, cultivating scriptural truths in his heart. He will climb onto my lap each morning before school so we can pray together, and we will discuss God's promises. One Scripture that is now embedded in his memory from these times is Philippians 4:13: *"I can do all things through* [Christ] *who strengthens me."*

What specifically am I cultivating in my grandson? What am I preparing him to hear in his mind for the rest of his life? Well, he wants to grow up and work for NASA, but to do something like that, he will have to work hard. He will need to prepare and train first by doing incredibly well in math and science. He will need to develop a robust work ethic. He also absolutely must stay away from drugs and alcohol. To help him, I cultivate the ground; I prepare him for this reality. I nurture and care for him and for his dreams.

When a farmer cultivates a field, he must be diligent to find and remove rocks. The first rock that shows up in that field of cultivating my grandson? I'm taking it out. What might that rock look like? Maybe it's a lie he is believing from culture or from Satan. Maybe it is a bad habit he has picked up that could turn into a character flaw. Whatever that rock might be, it needs to come out. The goal is to be attentive and to help lovingly remove it.

WHEN A FARMER CULTIVATES A FIELD, HE MUST BE DILIGENT TO FIND AND REMOVE ROCKS. THE FIRST ROCK THAT SHOWS UP IN THAT FIELD OF CULTIVATING MY GRANDSON? I'M TAKING IT OUT.

Weeds are another thing farmers must be on the lookout for, and we must be just as vigilant as we cultivate our kids. When weeds grow up, I'm pulling them, poisoning them, and burning them. I'm getting rid of those suckers! The best preventative measure against weeds is a lush and fertile field with a flourishing crop; in a healthy field, there is simply no room for weeds. An occasional weed might still grow up among the crop, and when we see it, we must remove it right away. Don't let the enemy sow anything into the field of your child's heart.

We must nurture and care for our kids in this way, cultivating them with the good things they need to grow well. Some of them will grow up as big as oak trees, some as dwarf trees, some as Japanese maples. No matter what the Lord has planned for them to grow into, we must always understand the need for them to have good soil, abundant water, and plenty of sunlight along the way.

I love the analogy of oak trees. There are big oaks and little oaks, big acorns and little acorns. With the right conditions, an acorn can one day grow into a mighty oak, in the same way that our kids can one day grow into mature men and women of God. We are responsible for cultivating them, for helping to ensure they get the nutrients and sun and water they need along the way.

We are all farmers in the kingdom of God. We are always in the cultivating stage, and we are all being cultivated. Jesus said, *"But seek first the kingdom of God and his righteousness, and all these things will be added to you"* (Matthew 6:33). What exactly are *"these things"*? They are right desires, and when we, as adults, have right desires, the young people in our sphere of influence will want what we have. They will want to be like us. Whatever tree we are, they will want to grow to be the same. They will come right alongside us as we walk with the Lord, and as they see our smiles and our blessings, they will want what we have, as well.

WITH THE RIGHT CONDITIONS, AN ACORN CAN ONE DAY GROW INTO A MIGHTY OAK, IN THE SAME WAY THAT OUR KIDS CAN ONE DAY GROW INTO MATURE MEN AND WOMEN OF GOD.

So let us cultivate first our own lives, our own ground. Our kids are going to come behind us, so let's give them something good to emulate. Let's plant seeds of hope, water them, and cultivate them in our young people so we can watch them grow.

NO CONDEMNATION

When we see kids going astray, we are often quick to condemn, but I would encourage you to first consider their family background. Until you know how they are being cultivated, by what values and by which caretakers, withhold your condemnation. Remember, we are all being cultivated, by one thing or another. If a young person is not being cultivated by good things, we should not be surprised to see bad fruit. Instead of condemning them, we can have a spirit of compassion for them.

As you begin to understand the cultivating stage, you may also be tempted to condemn yourself, to wallow in self-condemnation as you think about mistakes you have made. Don't do it! *"There is therefore now no condemnation for those who are in Christ Jesus"* (Romans 8:1). Remember that you can always dig up the ground and start fresh. God throws our sins into the sea of forgetfulness (see Micah 7:19) and removes our sins from us *"as far as the east is from the west"* (Psalm 103:12). If the Lord no longer condemns those who are in Christ, who are we to condemn ourselves? Christ's sacrifice on the cross is enough. Not only that, but in His grace, as part of our sanctification, He gives us fresh chances to repent and change. What we didn't do so well before, we can now approach differently with the Holy Spirit's help and with understanding from God's Word. We can cultivate in new ways—His ways.

IF THE LORD NO LONGER CONDEMNS
THOSE WHO ARE IN CHRIST, WHO ARE WE TO
CONDEMN OURSELVES? CHRIST'S SACRIFICE ON
THE CROSS IS ENOUGH.

Cultivating is nothing but work, and the stakes are too high to leave it to chance. We will cultivate in one way or another by the lives that we lead and by the instruction that we give—by our good teaching or by our wrong teaching. Know God and cling to Him, and then be attentive to the garden God has entrusted to your care.

TWO

LIFE'S TRAIN

If you've ever taken a long train ride, you know you usually cannot see the engineer, yet you put your faith in him. He is the one who knows how to drive the thing. Your job is to sit tight, enjoy the scenery, and get out once the train stops. The train may go through tunnels, across downhill grades, and between beautiful passes. You may not always know whether you are going up or down, but you will see and enjoy the scenery around you. The key to being able to enjoy that ride is knowing that you can trust the one in the locomotive. The same holds true in life. When we know God is our heavenly Engineer, we can enjoy the ride.

WHEN WE KNOW GOD IS OUR HEAVENLY
ENGINEER, WE CAN ENJOY THE RIDE.

THE POWER OF HABITS

One of the hardest things for a train to do is get going. The second most difficult thing for it to do is stop. The same is true for us; we can get into habits that cause an upward trajectory or a downward spiral, and it can be very hard to stop bad habits and replace them with good ones.

According to a 2009 study, it can take someone anywhere from 18 to 254 days to form a new habit, with most people taking right around 66 days.[3] That's more than two months! This means that if you are looking to form a new pattern that improves your lifestyle, you may have a tough time initially. Whether you are trying to stay away from substances, develop a healthy diet, or study harder for school, it will take time. Eventually your new lifestyle will become automatic, but the beginning phase is going to be tricky.

It takes time to develop new habits, and it also takes time to break the effects of addictive substances. Most addiction rehabilitation facilities offer 90-day treatment options because they recognize that the brain needs time to reset itself and shake off the physical influences of the addictive substance. If someone is in a recovery program, trained facilitators will suggest new habits that can make this phase less painful and to help ensure a more successful recovery.

When it comes to the body, the most important new habits revolve around exercise, diet, and sleep. These habits, which are crucial to recovery, are likewise powerful in helping us feel and think our best and thus reduce the allure of addictive substances and prevent the need for recovery in the first place.

EXERCISE

Regular exercise releases endorphins, which improve a person's state of mind. This can be powerful for the person trying to break an addiction and likewise powerful in preventing addiction in the first place. Exercising outdoors is especially helpful since sunlight helps release serotonin, which induces feelings of calm and focus.[4] No one should be forced to choose an exercise that

3. Phillippa Lally et al., "How Are Habits Formed: Modelling Habit Formation in the Real World," *European Journal of Social Psychology* 40, no. 6 (2010): 998-1009, https://doi.org/10.1002/ejsp.674.
4. Randy A. Sansone and Lori A. Sansone, "Sunshine, Serotonin, and Skin: A Partial Explanation for Seasonal Patterns in Psychopathology?" *Innovations in Clinical Neuroscience* (July–August 2013): 20–24, https://www.ncbi.nlm.nih.gov/pmc/articles/PMC3779905/#.

feels like a chore. Instead, people should choose activities that they find relaxing, enjoyable, and inspiring. This could include walking outdoors, hiking in the mountains, or going for a swim. Recovering addicts need to look forward to their active time. Once they begin to feel overworked, they should rest so that they won't feel turned off from this good habit that they're trying to establish. These same principles hold true for anyone trying to establish the regular habit of exercise.

DIET

A healthy diet high in vitamins is also important. Poultry and fish, for example, contain amino acids, which have been found to contribute to a sense of well-being.[5] Berries are another power-house, packed with antioxidants that can keep our bodies operating at their best. Take time to collect recipes and enjoy the process of preparing meals. It can be a fun experience; it doesn't have to be a chore.

Go ahead and give young people some choices when it comes to what they eat. Ask them which foods they like. What would they enjoy learning how to cook and then eat? The time spent working together in the kitchen can be a wonderful opportunity to connect while doing something that needs to be done anyway. During that time, you could listen to praise music and worship God together, all while moving toward better health. Eventually, as this foundation is laid, preparing and eating tasty, nutritious food will become a way of life for you and your kids, and you won't have to think twice about it because the habit will have been formed.

Closely related to diet is good hydration. Recovering addicts should keep water or seltzer close by for drinking at all times, and

5. Kentaro Umeda, Daichi Shindo, Shinji Somekawa, Shinobu Nishitani, Wataru Sato, Sakiko Toyoda, Sachise Karakawa, Mika Kawasaki, Tomoyuki Mine, and Katsuya Suzuki, "Effects of Five Amino Acids (Serine, Alanine, Glutamate, Aspartate, and Tyrosine) on Mental Health in Healthy Office Workers: A Randomized, Double-Blind, Placebo-Controlled Exploratory Trial," *Nutrients* (June 6, 2022): 14, https://pubmed.ncbi.nlm.nih.gov/35684157/.

this holds true for everyone hoping to feel their best. Hydration helps bodies to heal properly and keeps them from tiring out. Also, the faster a person can flush out the toxins that have built up through substance abuse, the better, and drinking water helps in that process more than anything else.

SLEEP

A healthy sleep schedule is vital, and this includes falling asleep and waking up at the same times each day. Find a good bedtime routine, and consider reading or taking a warm bath before going to bed. The Bible says, *"It is in vain that you rise up early and go late to rest, eating the bread of anxious toil; for he gives to his beloved sleep"* (Psalm 127:2). When people are addicted to substances, it often causes their sleep schedules to go haywire and throws off their natural sleep cycles. God has created us with the need to stop every day and recharge through rest and sleep. He loves us and wants us to rest. For example, in the psalms, we read, *"He makes me lie down in green pastures....He restores my soul"* (Psalm 23:2–3).

GOD HAS CREATED US WITH THE NEED
TO STOP EVERY DAY AND RECHARGE THROUGH
REST AND SLEEP. HE LOVES US AND
WANTS US TO REST.

HABITS FOR THE HEART AND MIND

In addition to habits that help build a healthy body, there are habits we can develop to transform our hearts and minds. Support groups, for example, can be life-changing, especially if they are Christ centered. Brothers and sisters in Christ who have been through similar struggles will be able to relate to each other and walk through those struggles together. Many of these groups can be found online. There might even be one in your area similar to the group I run. It is important to find a Christian group, however, because it will be able to give you something other groups cannot offer by helping you to stay in touch with our heavenly Engineer. When you know the One who is driving the train, you'll get where you need to be!

Reading is another good habit to develop, as it is a free source of entertainment that exercises the brain and makes a person more knowledgeable. It can also reduce stress and inspire a person. Individuals may also pick up other hobbies to develop new skills and stay balanced. Woodworking, fishing, and drawing can be soothing habits that may boost a person's mood while providing meaningful outlets for creativity. I encourage folks to spend an hour or two on these or other good habits each day, and see how they enrich their lives and keep them from spending time on things that are life draining.

INSTILLING GOOD HABITS IN OUR CHILDREN

The skills and healthy habits discussed so far in this chapter are all critical for the person in recovery, but they are also critical foundational habits that can help prevent the need for recovery in the first place! When it comes to your family, you need to start early in cultivating good habits. Make sure your kids understand what is expected of them. Clearly communicate what the consequences will be if they don't obey—and don't be afraid to enforce them. Our heavenly Father is always gentle and forgiving with us, but He is not in the business of rescuing us from the consequences of our poor decisions if that's what it takes to teach us an important lesson. We should parent our children likewise. Sometimes painful consequences help drive the lesson home.

MAKE SURE YOUR KIDS UNDERSTAND
WHAT IS EXPECTED OF THEM. CLEARLY
COMMUNICATE WHAT THE CONSEQUENCES WILL
BE IF THEY DON'T OBEY—AND DON'T BE
AFRAID TO ENFORCE THEM.

Instruct your children to respect those in authority. Teach them good manners. Find enriching activities you enjoy doing together, perhaps exploring nature or painting on canvas. Set an example for your children in terms of following God's law, even when it's difficult, and be involved in your church community, as children will remember this when they are older.

Even if you do not struggle with substance addiction, keep up good habits with the body God has blessed you with. Stay physically active, since that will reduce anxiety and depression and make it easier for you to manage daily challenges. Eat healthily, as that will help you feel your best and also help prevent all kinds of physical problems, including obesity, diabetes, and heart disease. Give yourself a chance to develop the kind of positive self-image that your heavenly Father has always desired you to have.

GIVE IT TIME

Getting rid of poor habits, whether they are related to substance abuse or not, requires time. Accept that there will be a bit of an adjustment period. You may have fallen into a bad habit, such as criticizing yourself, getting disorganized, or being sedentary. When you first try to break these habits, it won't seem natural. It may be hard, and you might find yourself about to fall right back into old patterns. It's going to take a lot of effort and deliberate self-discipline to get up off the couch or to declutter that closet. Keep at it. You can do this. And to help you along the way, be sure you are spending time with your heavenly Father and with other

Christians. That is key. You need others to lean on along the way, to help make the journey easier and to give you encouragement.

YOU NEED OTHERS TO LEAN ON ALONG THE WAY, TO HELP MAKE THE JOURNEY EASIER AND TO GIVE YOU ENCOURAGEMENT.

Once you establish a healthy pattern, you will find that doing the right thing does not take as much effort. After a good habit is in place, you may even look forward to it. Starting your day with a walk or ending your day with a good book before bedtime will become activities you look forward to. Do this, and you will find a key to unlocking God's plans for your future. You must make doing the right thing—even when you don't want to—part of your character, and the Lord will bless you by changing the desires of your heart.

KNOW YOUR ENGINEER

You alone can answer the question of who is driving your train, and the same holds true for our kids. Who's driving the train? A boyfriend or girlfriend? A parent? A teacher? Whose voice is speaking inside your head when you're making important decisions? Who do you most want to be like?

Some kids grow up in a fatherless home, and others grow up with a fatherless heart. They feel as if no one is interested in who they are or how they will turn out. Still others waste their lives trying to please parents who will never be happy with them. The good news is that we as believers have a perfect Father. He is never mean, harsh, or unfeeling. He does not push us around. He knows everything we have been through and all that we desire, and He doesn't hold it against us.

WE AS BELIEVERS HAVE A PERFECT FATHER.
HE KNOWS EVERYTHING WE HAVE BEEN
THROUGH AND ALL OUR DESIRES DESIRE, AND
HE DOESN'T HOLD IT AGAINST US.

How do you make sure He's in the driver's seat of your life? The first thing you need to do is begin listening to Him. We have so many voices in our lives, and it is easy for one or more of them to drown out the gentle calling of the One who loves us. Hearing from Him will require regular, honest seeking. Make an effort every day to spend time with the One who loves you.

You do not have to be a Bible scholar to get to know God. Find a chapter of Scripture to read each day and a devotional you enjoy. Pray for a few minutes and just thank God for what you have.

Sometimes the train of life is humming along nicely, and you just sit back and take in what you see. There are days when you need to look out the window and thank God for the hills and the trees and the wild animals. Your trip may be filled with sunlight one day and clouds the next, but you can be thankful for where you are right now.

The next time you are feeling down, turn to God first. Try going to your knees. Corrie ten Boom once said, "The wonderful thing about praying is that you leave a world of not being able to do something, and enter God's realm where everything is possible. He specializes in the impossible. Nothing is too great for His almighty power. Nothing is too small for His love."[6] Pray when you feel desperate, and pray when you don't feel like it. God is there, and you will get answers.

Keeping a journal is another way to connect with your heavenly Father. You can keep track of your prayers and when they are answered. Write down Bible verses that speak to you. Journaling

6. Corrie ten Boom, *I Stand at the Door and Knock: Meditations by the Author of the Hiding Place* (Grand Rapids: Zondervan, 2008), 95.

will help keep a record of your thoughts, dreams, and progress. When you feel like falling back into bad habits, read a few pages from your journal and remember what God has already brought you through. It will remind you how far you already have come.

THE NEXT TIME YOU ARE FEELING DOWN, TURN TO GOD FIRST. TRY GOING TO YOUR KNEES.

If you are serious about following the heavenly Engineer, you also need to spend time with His children. Are you part of a support group at church that nurtures you? Can you tell them your hopes and prayers without fear that you'll be gossiped about? Will they counsel you in grace and truth? The walk of a serious Christian is not one you can do alone. You need others who can support you when you feel unable. Praying, worshipping, and learning are all group activities made stronger by fellowship with other believers.

ENJOYING THE RIDE

With God as your Engineer, you can rest easy. Jesus said,

Come to me, all who labor and are heavy laden, and I will give you rest. Take my yoke upon you, and learn from me, for I am gentle and lowly in heart, and you will find rest for your souls. For my yoke is easy, and my burden is light.
(Matthew 11:28–30)

The train will protect you when it's raining, and it will get you where you're dreaming of going. Good kids go bad because no one introduces them to the Engineer. Once they meet Him, they can chug along happily the way they were meant to.

Those who are enjoying the ride are invested in positive relationships with people they can trust. They go out for coffee and talk about what's really going on. They enjoy hanging out with those who are real, those who share both their struggles and their victories. They learn and grow every day alongside people who comfort and inspire them.

People who enjoy the ride do not waste time regretting the past, complaining about the present, or dreading the future. The apostle Paul said, *"But one thing I do: forgetting what lies behind and straining forward to what lies ahead, I press on toward the goal for the prize of the upward call of God in Christ Jesus"* (Philippians 3:13–14). People who enjoy the ride are ready for what the future holds. It may be a job opportunity or a wonderful relationship or a lovely trip to the mountains, but they press on to what God has called them to.

PEOPLE WHO ENJOY THE RIDE DO NOT WASTE TIME REGRETTING THE PAST, COMPLAINING ABOUT THE PRESENT, OR DREADING THE FUTURE.

Individuals enjoying life's train ride understand the importance of balance. There will be time for work, time for socializing, and time for just gazing at the sky with your hands behind your head. You will take in the wonder of creation along the way and remember that you are one of your Creator's most treasured beings, traveling through His wonderful world on your way to where He's called you.

THREE

ROCKS DREAM OF NOTHING

When children have a fatherless heart, they are in danger of growing up without dreams. When their home life is not inspiring, encouraging, or edifying, their future seems bleak and cold. Jonathan Edwards once wrote that if we are to understand the concept of "nothing," we "must think of *the same that the sleeping rocks dream of*; and not till then shall we get a complete idea of *nothing*" (emphasis added).[7] Of course, none of us is like a rock, dreaming of nothing. Our minds are abuzz. It is human for us to dream, to plan, and to have visions for our futures.

> NONE OF US IS LIKE A ROCK, DREAMING OF
> NOTHING. OUR MINDS ARE ABUZZ. IT IS HUMAN
> FOR US TO DREAM, TO PLAN, AND TO HAVE
> VISIONS FOR OUR FUTURES.

Our children are not rocks. They are prone to dreaming, just like all humans. The problem is that many kids do not understand the nature of dreaming *and* going after our dreams. Instead of envisioning their future and making plans to get there, many

7. Jonathan Edwards, "The Idea of Being Nothing," from "Of Being," in *Library of the World's Best Literature, Ancient and Modern*, ed. Charles Dudley Warner (New York: R. S. Peale and J. A. Hill, 1896), 13:5183, https://www.gutenberg.org/files/34408/34408-h/34408-h.htm (accessed December 26, 2023).

young people look downtrodden these days because they have lofty goals but no road maps to reach them. Many teens dream of becoming NBA stars or astronauts or Internet influencers. Their dreams begin as unrealistic ships on the horizon that change shape as they get closer.

Maybe they won't grow up to be NBA stars, but they can play for the school basketball team and coach when they get older. Perhaps they won't become astronauts, but they can go to school to become engineers. They may not grow up to be Internet influencers, but they can influence those around them for the sake of the kingdom. These attainable dreams—and the plans to get there—give our kids reasons for getting up in the morning, purposes beyond just getting through the day.

The opposite is also true. When young people do not have achievable dreams they can work toward, they will become aimless, purposeless. Each day will feel like a nightmare as they struggle just to make it through. This is when the danger of becoming dependent on substances is high as they look for something to fill the voids in their hearts, and this is why it is important for young people to have something to dream about that has the potential to become a reality.

God has given each of us the ultimate calling of glorifying Him, but the way we live out that calling will look different from person to person. It is a joy and an honor to figure that out, to identify specifically *how* to glorify God as we go about our days, *how* to live life well, *how* to serve Him through our work, *how* to leave our mark on this earth. These things are all part of our purpose, and it is never too early for kids to start thinking about their purpose. Most kids will not know what their final purpose is yet, but pursuing good things now will ultimately grow into what they will do someday.

GOD HAS GIVEN EACH OF US THE ULTIMATE
CALLING OF GLORIFYING HIM, BUT THE WAY WE
LIVE OUT THAT CALLING WILL LOOK DIFFERENT
FROM PERSON TO PERSON.

INSPIRING OUR CHILDREN

As I mentioned earlier, my son suffers from a traumatic brain injury, but he is still following his dream and living out his purpose. Every day he gets up, sees the mountains, and goes fishing. If I'm honest, I see ways that, as a parent, I could have done more to help my son physically, spiritually, or financially, areas in which perhaps I was a stumbling block in his life. Most parents probably feel this way to some degree, but it is important that we do not dwell here and beat ourselves up. Ultimately, the responsibility for his life belongs to my son, and by God's grace he has overcome through the blood of the Lamb and by the power of his testimony (see Revelation 12:11).

Although we should never beat ourselves up, it is good to learn from our mistakes and to strive to do better. If we know we have not encouraged our children as much as we should have, it is never too late to start! As parents, we often recognize the seed of something in our children that longs to blossom into something more. We can encourage, water, and nurture those seeds.

For instance, think of a child who comes home from school having drawn a picture she is quite proud of. This same child spends a lot of time perfecting anything visual in her life, including the layout of her room or a sandcastle on the beach. Everything has to be just so, and she spends hours looking for just the right colors or accessories to complement her creations. This child has a natural affinity for art, and her parents can help nurture that affinity by praising and encouraging her.

Praise is a free and simple way to let your children know that you see what they are good at and that you admire their talent. Praise can go a long way toward bolstering our children's confidence and encouraging them to continue honing their crafts. It can help them think positively about themselves in a world that is constantly seeking to tear them down.

PRAISE IS A FREE AND SIMPLE WAY TO
LET YOUR CHILDREN KNOW THAT YOU SEE
WHAT THEY ARE GOOD AT AND THAT YOU
ADMIRE THEIR TALENT.

When you feel proud of your children, tell them. Maybe your son made a valiant effort with a difficult school assignment, or maybe your daughter was kind to another student when no one else was. Let them know that you saw their good work, and praise them for it. If they feel like no one notices, they may be tempted to withdraw. Bring them out of their shells by praising what they have done well and by showing them that you noticed.

WHEN TO REWARD

Praise can be reinforced through rewards. These do not need to be expensive, but they should be meaningful. For example, let's say your daughter earns an A on a report she worked hard on, or your son brought in the winning run at the Little League baseball game. An ice cream cone or a trip to your local fast-food joint to get a burger together might be all the reward needed to celebrate their accomplishments. Be sure to tell your kids you are proud of them and their hard work.

In today's world of competition and cruelty, it is easy for kids to become discouraged. Parents can help counter this through the 4:1 ratio of positive-to-negative reinforcement, a concept that is popular with educators and others who work with children. All children need discipline and correction sometimes, but for every one of these discipline moments, we should strive to give four positive comments. Be on the lookout for the little things your kids do right, and praise them for those! Let them know you're proud that they took out the garbage without complaining or that they woke up for school on time without being told. It may seem unnecessary to praise our children for such simple things, but they are constantly fighting against an enemy seeking to tear them to pieces. Praising them is a small thing we can do to bolster their confidence and help them overcome feelings of discouragement.

ALL CHILDREN NEED DISCIPLINE AND
CORRECTION SOMETIMES, BUT FOR EVERY ONE
OF THESE DISCIPLINE MOMENTS, WE SHOULD
STRIVE TO GIVE FOUR POSITIVE COMMENTS.

Supporting your children's dreams financially is another way you can help counter the attacks of the devil. This can be tricky, as many parents struggle to put food on the table, yet investing in your child's dream could be the difference between a bleak future and one streaked with rays of light. Does your child have a gift for music that you could nurture with regular lessons from a qualified teacher? Should you be paying a fee for them to sign up for the local basketball league? Can you take them on a trip to a museum so they will get to see what quality paintings look like?

These kinds of opportunities may require some sacrifices on your part—perhaps getting a second job to pay for lessons, forgoing a fancy family vacation to free up funds for activities, or driving out of your way each week so your child can study with a great teacher—but these types of sacrifices are worth it if it means stoking the fire of your children's dreams. In the future, you will reap the rewards of these investments through their mental and emotional well-being.

SPIRITUAL ENCOURAGEMENT

As Christians we also know the value of supporting our children spiritually and helping to nurture spiritual health within them. As kids get older, there will be disappointing moments that could discourage them. They might drop the ball at a baseball game or lose a singing contest they had hoped to win. They could be rejected by someone they wanted to date or hurt by people they thought were their friends. These are normal parts of growing up that can devastate sensitive kids. Words of affirmation from their parents are important in these seasons but may fall short in helping kids to get back up on their feet.

It is crucial that our children know they have a heavenly Father they can depend on. Point them to their Father! Jeremiah 29:11 says, *"For I know the plans I have for you, declares the LORD, plans for welfare and not for evil, to give you a future and a hope."* Young people need to know that setbacks do not mean the end of the road. Their heavenly Father sees their struggles, and He wants them to accomplish His purposes in their lives. He wants what is best for them, and He will walk with them through the hard stuff.

IT IS CRUCIAL THAT OUR CHILDREN KNOW THEY
HAVE A HEAVENLY FATHER THEY CAN DEPEND
ON. POINT THEM TO THEIR FATHER!

Our children will eventually grow up and leave home. When they are on their own, they can still have a Parent who loves them and directs them toward a positive future. As earthly parents, we should teach them to rely on their heavenly Father. For instance, we can encourage them to pray when they are discouraged, and we can model this behavior ourselves. We can give them age-appro-priate devotional books and teach them to spend time in the Word each day. We can also take them to a church where they can grow and be mentored by individuals who have overcome struggles like their own.

Most of all, we need to be the kinds of adults who model patience, forgiveness, and righteousness. Our kids are watching us. Will we be models of Chrisitan love and holiness, or will they see something else in our lives? When our kids realize that hope is possible, they will begin to develop a positive outlook, and they will be unafraid of a future full of uncertainty, recognizing that it is also ripe with possibility.

OUR KIDS ARE WATCHING US. WILL WE BE MODELS OF CHRISITAN LOVE AND HOLINESS, OR WILL THEY SEE SOMETHING ELSE IN OUR LIVES?

FINDING A DREAM

How do we help our children find their dreams? For some kids it is obvious from a young age where they are gifted, but for others it is not. It is important for us to expose our kids to different types of activities so they can get a feel for what they like and what they are good at. Your child's teachers will likely help point out any gifting or inclination they observe for athletics, academics, or the arts. Talk to these professionals about what they think your child's strengths may be.

Some young people are wonderful at planting flowers, build-ing things, or working with younger children, skills they may not necessarily get to practice during school hours. Helping your child discover these talents can be tricky, so don't be afraid to think outside the box. Your child might be able to work on a local farm, take a class at a local hardware store, or volunteer in your church's Sunday school program. Be sure to praise your child if they seem to have a real talent for something, and give them opportunities to do more with that gift. It will work wonders for their self-esteem, all while helping to prepare them for their purpose in life.

Your children may also let you know how they are gifted by what makes them excited. For example, your daughter might start packing for a backpacking trip well in advance because she is so eager to go. Or your son might spend hours trying to perfect his piano piece. These are good indicators that those activities motivate and inspire them. When kids feel confident that they can achieve excellence, they are willing to put in extra effort. Be on the lookout for areas where your kids are working joyfully and diligently; very often, these turn out to be areas of gifting.

BE ON THE LOOKOUT FOR AREAS WHERE YOUR KIDS ARE WORKING JOYFULLY AND DILIGENTLY; VERY OFTEN, THESE TURN OUT TO BE AREAS OF GIFTING.

On the other hand, if your child dreads something, that may be an indicator his gifting lies elsewhere. If your kid dreads soccer practice or becomes pouty every time he must practice his instrument, those probably are not his strengths. This does not mean children automatically should be excused from doing things they don't like. There is great value in teaching kids discipline and perseverance through unpleasant experiences. At the same time, we can use these natural inclinations as guideposts for what God may or may not be calling them to do for the rest of their lives.

MAKE A GAME PLAN

The more time our young people spend pursuing their dreams, the less nightmarish their adult lives will be. As children get older, it is important for them to have not only vision for their future but also game plans to help make those dreams reality. These plans should be more practical than wishful. This is not to say that kids cannot dream big but rather that their goals should be realistic and attainable.

THE MORE TIME OUR YOUNG PEOPLE
SPEND PURSUING THEIR DREAMS, THE LESS
NIGHTMARISH THEIR ADULT LIVES WILL BE.

For example, a young person may have dreamed of becoming a football star. This may no longer be possible because an injury has made professional sports an impossibility, but he may still be able to teach at a local school and coach his favorite team on the side. Or maybe your child has always dreamed of starting her own business. Could she begin apprenticing with a local plumber, electrician, or chef to see what the job entails? Is there somewhere she could get certification for the type of work she would like to do?

Young people who are excited about their futures will be less enthusiastic about the types of immediate gratification that drugs and alcohol promise. Addiction comes easily, and it will always come after young people. They need to put themselves in the right place and listen to people who will encourage and inspire them. They can find a group of like-minded individuals at church who can pray with them in their struggles and take a genuine interest in their well-being.

When God puts a dream in a young person's heart, He also gives that young person the authority, the power, and the strength to carry it out. This means that if a young person's plan is from our heavenly Father, it will not fail. Begin praying for that dream to take root today. We can overcome each day through a life surrendered to Jesus.

WHEN GOD PUTS A DREAM IN A YOUNG PERSON'S
HEART, HE ALSO GIVES THAT YOUNG PERSON
THE AUTHORITY, THE POWER, AND THE
STRENGTH TO CARRY IT OUT.

This does not mean that dreams come easily. In fact, following a dream can be the hardest thing a person does, with fears, rejections, and setbacks along the way. Sometimes there are hurdles that seem insurmountable until God provides a way over them, but He will provide a way. As parents of young people, we are called to encourage our children in wholesome dreams that will help them make the world a better place. If we continue in faith, love, and good works, our time on earth will have been well spent, and will be well rewarded.

FOUR

SELF-WORTH
VERSUS SELF-ESTEEM

When you think of someone who has low self-esteem, do you envision the stereotypical poor slob trudging along with his head down, feeling like he's blown it and no one will ever like him? Our society values self-esteem and holds in high regard those who have favorable opinions of themselves. The Bible, however, has a few things to say about this.

Before I go any further, let me pause and point out that there is a critical distinction between *self-worth* and *self-esteem*. *Merriam-Webster's Dictionary* defines self-esteem as "a confidence and satisfaction in oneself."[8] Self-esteem has to be earned. When people have low self-esteem, they're going to have to work to build it up. They might lose some weight, go to the gym, or start a business. They may need to take career aptitude tests and figure out how they can become successful professionally. Self-esteem requires us to come up with a plan and stick to it, overcome obstacles, and make responsible decisions. It demands that we know where we are headed and that we defeat the temptation to be lazy.

Self-esteem has its place in our children's lives, and it *is* part of our duty as caregivers to instill in our kids' habits that will pay

---

8. *Merriam-Webster.com Dictionary*, s.v. "self-esteem," accessed December 26, 2023, https://www.merriam-webster.com/dictionary/self-esteem.

off later in higher self-esteem. We can teach them to eat right, to save their money, to complete their schoolwork on time. We can help them hone their interests and talents so that they can help make the world a bit better. When young people are healthy and successful, they will naturally have a stronger self-image and better self-esteem.

The problem with self-esteem, however, is that it can vanish in an instant. Our kids might suddenly be hit with the notion that they've messed up or done something they can't be proud of, and if they don't understand their *self-worth*, they can quickly plummet down the rabbit hole of self-destruction. Self-worth is different from self-esteem because it does not depend upon our actions. Instead, it comes from our heavenly Father. No matter how much weight you gain or how many quizzes you fail or how many business startups don't succeed, you can still have self-worth.

God doesn't love us because of who we are. He loves because of who He is. As humans, we know we will often fail to reach our goals, yet something inside us longs to be loved unconditionally. The acceptance of a forgiving God provides that unconditional love and sense of self-worth in ways that the world cannot, and nothing can take that away from us.

GOD DOESN'T LOVE US BECAUSE OF WHO WE
ARE. HE LOVES BECAUSE OF WHO HE IS.

INVESTING ETERNALLY

As I've gotten older, retirement has become a popular subject of discussion among my peers. People are always asking questions like, "What kind of pension do you have?" or, "Do you have a 401(k)?" or, "When does your Medicaid kick in?" Some of my friends want to know how I'm going to secure my future when my hands stop working and can no longer lay bricks, and most of them are facing similar questions in their own lives.

As Christians, we need to be prepared for our *eternal* retirement. We cannot measure this in money or in the praises of others or in human wisdom. Instead, we must ask ourselves about the reward in heaven that is waiting for us. Trials and tribulations in life are inevitable. People we thought we could trust will let us down, and we will experience disappointments and depression. The only way to turn this around is through a life surrendered to God and His Word. We must know where our true worth is found if we are going to make it.

As parents, we can do plenty of things to help kids understand their self-worth. We can compliment them on their strengths frequently and avoid dishing out harsh criticism. We can encourage kids to be more independent and give them plenty of chances to show off work and accomplishments that they are proud of. Most of all, we can point them to the One who loves them unconditionally. No one is on this earth by accident, and God has important work for our children to do. He considers them so valuable that He sent His only Son to die in their place so that they could follow Him to heaven one day. Our children need to know these truths.

We need to uphold the unchanging nature of our children's self-worth intentionally in our homes every day. Do we berate our children and shame them every time they make a mistake? Are we prone to resurrecting past errors and reminding them later of things they have done wrong? Or do we patiently talk to them about what they can learn from their mistakes, assuring them that they are still loved? Do our children know that, even as we correct them, we love them and accept them unconditionally?

DO OUR CHILDREN KNOW THAT, EVEN AS WE
CORRECT THEM, WE LOVE THEM AND ACCEPT
THEM UNCONDITIONALLY?

Many parents mistakenly believe that they are disciplining their children when in fact they are simply insulting or demeaning them. The Bible warns us that the tongue is like a rudder that can control the whole course of our lives, as well as a fire that can bring great destruction:

> *Look at the ships also: though they are so large and are driven by strong winds, they are guided by a very small rudder wherever the will of the pilot directs. So also the tongue is a small member, yet it boasts of great things. How great a forest is set ablaze by such a small fire! And the tongue is a fire, a world of unrighteousness. The tongue is set among our members, staining the whole body, setting on fire the entire course of life, and set on fire by hell.* (James 3:4–6)

Our tongues are powerful. The things we say to our children can cut them to the quick and immediately defeat them, or they can spur them on toward righteousness and good deeds. As adults, we must be aware of the kind of power we have with our words—and use it responsibly.

While it is important for young people to understand that certain behaviors are not acceptable, parents must be careful not to cross the line and correct their children to the point of wounding them emotionally. If you want your children to grow up with healthy self-confidence, allow them to see the love of God modeled in you. This means being willing to correct and admonish your children when you see them veering off course but also being eager to encourage them and let them know you believe the very best of them. Our heavenly Father does not give up on us when we fail, and we should reflect that patient love in how we parent the children He has put in our care.

WORDS TO BUILD UP

The Bible has much to say about using our words to build others up rather than tearing them down. Hearing and digesting negative words can be detrimental to a child, and this can mean the difference between a positive life and one that is devastated by a single wrong turn.

Scripture instructs us, *"Let no corrupting talk come out of your mouths, but only such as is good for building up, as fits the occasion, that it may give grace to those who hear"* (Ephesians 4:29). We know how critical it is to the spiritual lives of others to speak words that will uplift them. As caregivers, this sometimes can be difficult, but it is no less important. We might be upset that our children are not listening, or we may grow frustrated with their desire to have things their way, yet there are always avenues of spurring them on in good works. Did your child share a snack or toy with a friend today or perhaps notice and reach out to a friend who was upset? When you see your kids doing good things, make sure you compliment them on their willingness to step out of their own world and demonstrate kindness.

The Bible tells us, *"A joyful heart is good medicine, but a crushed spirit dries up the bones"* (Proverbs 17:22). Our children's peers have plenty to say that can bring them down. Young people can be quick to mock and tease when someone says or does something foolish. Add to that an academic failure at school or rejection by a potential boyfriend or girlfriend, and your child can easily experience a crushed spirit. Our children might even begin telling themselves that there is something wrong with them or that success is only a dream, which can lead to many problems in life, including physical ailments. As caregivers, we are in the unique position to restore joy to our children's souls. We should always be searching for opportunities to praise them. We can use Scripture to gently guide them rather than condemn, and we can let them know on a regular basis how valuable they are to their heavenly Father.

AS CAREGIVERS,
WE ARE IN THE UNIQUE POSITION TO RESTORE
JOY TO OUR CHILDREN'S SOULS.

Adults can also demonstrate optimism to children, showing them how to look on the bright side of any situation. For example, we can say, "I'm sorry we have to wait longer for our lunch, but this gives us a chance to spend more time together!" Kids can learn through watching us that we do not always have to wear our unhappiness on our sleeves, but that we can instead look for positives and try to make the best of the circumstances in which we find ourselves. We can help our kids understand that it is normal to face obstacles sometimes and that our confidence doesn't have to be shaken by it.

As a caregiver, you can pour yourself out for your children, but it is also important for young minds to be saturated with uplifting voices in addition to your own. If children are exposed to positive, life-affirming, gospel-centered words from a variety of fronts, they will begin to believe them. What kinds of messages are circling throughout your home when you aren't speaking? Are you playing encouraging Christian music, or are songs your child listens to replete with heartbreak, lust, and anger? How about the books your child reads? Do they reinforce good attitudes and Christian values, or do they idolize selfishness and worldly ideals? Does your child take time each day to hear the wonderful, encouraging messages of Scripture? Are there resources you can purchase that will make their Bible study more appealing and accessible?

Similarly, your children should be spending time with Christian friends who uplift and encourage them. Just because someone attends the same church as a youngster does not mean that person is a positive influence. Wise caregivers can discern those who will be encouragements for their kids. Are your children's friends consumed with dating, fashion, and foolhardy risk-taking, or are they committed to living for Jesus? Young people are easily influenced by their peers because they want to fit in. Look for peer groups where it is cool to be kind, respectful, and virtuous.

The village that will help you raise your child should also be brimming with folks who know that *they* have infinite worth in the eyes of their heavenly Father. Are your church leaders sour and self-righteous, or are they relaxed and enthusiastic about their own place in the kingdom? Young people learn a lot about how to behave from what they see. Make sure they have examples of adults who believe all things are possible through Him who gives them strength (see Philippians 4:13).

KNOWLEDGE AND SELF-ESTEEM

Individuals suffering from low self-esteem often try to compensate for this by gaining knowledge, which can lead to a damaging, haughty attitude toward others. The Bible tells us that *"'knowledge' puffs up, but love builds up"* (1 Corinthians 8:1). Knowledge is not a weapon to use against others, and there are many times when it is wiser for us not to share what we know but rather to focus on encouraging others in love.

Knowledge is not a bad thing in itself, of course. In fact, Christians should focus on gaining as much information as they can in order to be able to give reasons for their faith. Scripture tells us to *"always [be] prepared to make a defense to anyone who asks you for a reason for the hope that is in you"* (1 Peter 3:15). Some may believe that we blindly put our faith in the unseen, but we know that our minds are in agreement. The world has an order to it that can be explained through intelligent design, and the Scriptures are well attested to by both believing and unbelieving historians. We might be tempted to present facts in arrogance, however, and that can cause others to shut their ears. The remainder of 1 Peter 3:15 says that we are to give the defense for our faith *"with gentleness and respect."* Our knowledge must be accompanied by humility.

Remember, "*God opposes the proud but gives grace to the humble*" (James 4:6).

King Uzziah was a well-respected king of Judah who was crowned at only sixteen years of age, and he reigned for fifty-two years. He was righteous and sought the Lord, which led to great favor. He built armies and towers and defeated enemies. He listened to God's righteous prophet Zechariah, whose instruction was rooted in fear of the Lord. After Zechariah died, however, King Uzziah became consumed with pride. He attempted to burn incense on the altar at the temple, which was something only priests were allowed to do. Despite being warned by many priests, Uzziah entered the temple to make the sacrifice, and the Lord struck him with leprosy. He had to live a life in isolation from that point on, turning his kingdom over to the governance of his son.

Stories like that of Uzziah painfully illustrate that pride really does come before a fall. (See Proverbs 16:18.) We might be working with nothing but zeal for God's kingdom, yet success often brings with it a strong temptation to become proud. As you grow in wisdom, it is important to guard against pride taking root in your heart. God's way is still best, and disobeying Him can lead to great pain. As we seek to admonish those entrusted to our care, we must avoid lording it over them with our knowledge. Instead we should use our knowledge and wisdom to gently bring things up, imparting only as much truth as our listeners are ready to hear. When we know our children, we are aware of how much correction they will be able to handle at one time. Once they have begun to live according to God's law, we can begin bringing them even closer as we walk alongside them in their sanctification.

SUCCESS OFTEN BRINGS WITH IT A STRONG
TEMPTATION TO BECOME PROUD.

Self-worth rather than self-esteem is what we should be cultivating in the next generation. Every day we must remind our children of their inherent value in the kingdom of God. We can still impart practical solutions that will allow our children to have confident views of themselves—things like good study habits, consistent exercise routines, and daily practice to succeed. The need for understanding self-worth, however, is paramount since it is more important than self-esteem. Today's young people must know they are precious to their Savior, no matter what they have done, and that all can be made well if only they will go to Him for forgiveness. This confidence allows them to overcome any challenges they may face and correct any wrong turns they may take along the way.

FIVE

SETTING THE LAW

If you have ever seen police dogs on television or walking around city streets, you know they are not there just for show. They have an important job to do. These animals are indispensable for sniffing out drugs or weapons, locating missing people, and protecting innocent individuals. They are trained from the time they are puppies to follow commands, attack intruders, and recognize substances. The same holds true for the exotic animals we see in the circus, including lions, tigers, and monkeys. These beasts are wild in nature, but they are carefully trained to serve a specific purpose. Their upbringing curtails their natural impulses and teaches them to behave in ways that benefit others.

In a similar way, parents can establish the law at home to curtail the sinful tendencies of every child's spirit. Scripture instructs us, *"Train up a child in the way he should go; even when he is old he will not depart from it"* (Proverbs 22:6). Many children exhibit behavioral problems in school, and while explanations like ADD, ADHD, and bipolar disorder should not be ignored, we must also look carefully at the home environment. If we raise our children properly now, we give them tools like discipline and self-control that they can carry with them into adulthood, when the consequences for foolishness are far more serious.

SETTING THE RULES

Most parents understand that children need to be protected from certain natural tendencies so they will not bring harm to themselves or to others. We install baby gates by stairways, keep children away from stoves, and put covers on electrical outlets. When a kid is ready to ride a bike, we put training wheels on it until the child is old enough to balance the bike without assistance. We automatically understand the need to put these safeguards in place to protect our children physically.

We parents must also establish clear rules and consequences in the home to protect our children spiritually, intellectually, and emotionally. Often, this is easier said than done, as children will sometimes become quite angry and push back when rules are established. In the long run, however, such conflicts are worth the hassle. The Bible tells us, *"For the moment all discipline seems painful rather than pleasant, but later it yields the peaceful fruit of righteousness to those who have been trained by it"* (Hebrews 12:11). As Scripture confirms, disciplining children is difficult work, but the result—a son or daughter who is morally prepared to face life in a complicated world—makes it all worthwhile.

AS PARENTS, WE MUST ESTABLISH
CLEAR RULES AND CONSEQUENCES IN THE HOME
TO PROTECT OUR CHILDREN SPIRITUALLY,
INTELLECTUALLY, AND EMOTIONALLY.

The younger your children's ages when you start establishing rules for them, the better. As they grow older, they will begin to understand that their parents are wiser and more experienced, but in those early years, they may try to push against you and see what they can get away with. (Of course, older kids can still be prone to do this at times!) Be wary of continually shifting rules at the first sign of pushback. If your kids see you change the rules every time they complain about them, you will be training them in disobedience and undermining their growth in self-control. There may be times when course correction is needed, times when it makes sense to adjust household rules and expectations; but if you never follow through on consequences, you will not be doing your kids any favors.

Specifically, what kinds of rules should we be establishing in our homes? Each household will have different needs and unique circumstances, but there are a few key areas I would like to discuss where many parents are tempted to be lackadaisical and hands-off. Specifically, our children will benefit from clear guidance with regard to bedtimes, chores, screen privileges, and relating to others.

BEDTIME

Children, especially young children, will not want to go to sleep when you tell them, but you know they need sleep to function and have decent behavior during the day. A solid routine helps with this. Develop a predictable bedtime routine where you tell them a story before bed or sing them a song while they brush their teeth. This routine should happen at the same time every night with very few exceptions. Keep this time consistent, and the benefits of quality sleep will positively impact every aspect of your child's life. As they become adults, children who have developed good sleep habits will prioritize sleep so that they can be alert and amicable while tackling life's daily responsibilities.

CHORES

Children should have rules governing their daily chores, as well. Kids as young as preschool age can begin cleaning up their toys after they play. This is an important habit for them to develop since it teaches them responsibility and ownership. They will quickly realize they are capable of tidying up, which also will give them a sense of being "big kids" who are not dependent upon their parents for everything. Kids who are required to clean up after themselves quickly learn that the world is not full of grown-up servants ready to pick up their messes and cater to their needs. This builds appreciation and respect for those in authority and prevents kids from becoming pompous or feeling like they are above certain tasks. Instead they will realize they are an important part of caring for the world around them.

As your child gets older, you can add to their chore list, as well as to their sense of ownership and self-respect. For example, children as young as five or six may be able to make their own beds, empty trash cans, or clear the table. They can also bring in the mail, dust furniture, or fold their own clothes. This requires a bit of patience, as children often perform their chores in a less-than-perfect way initially, and you will need to train them how to best complete their tasks. In the end, however, your children will begin to learn that the mysterious world of adults is a place they can understand. They are capable of caring for themselves, and they don't need constant assistance. When your children become teens, they can even do their own laundry and prepare meals for the family. This will make starting life on their own a lot easier than it is for other young people who are accustomed to being waited on.

YOUR CHILDREN WILL BEGIN TO LEARN
THAT THE MYSTERIOUS WORLD OF ADULTS IS A
PLACE THEY CAN UNDERSTAND.

SCREENS

Don't be afraid to set limits in terms of screen time for both older and younger kids. Phones, video games, and TV shows are tempting, because they are spellbinding and can keep our kids quietly absorbed for hours at a time. When children become accustomed to being entertained constantly, they will struggle to keep their minds occupied in other ways. As parents, we know we can cook dinner, clean the house, and maybe even get some part-time work done while our kids are pulled into their electronic worlds. Too much screen time, however, can be detrimental to children. It can lead to behavioral problems, obesity, and sleep deprivation, which can cause even bigger physical and mental issues later in life. Additionally, the expedient nature of these activities decreases a kid's ability to focus and concentrate on difficult tasks.

Many devices today are equipped with features that allow parents to limit screen time or shut them off at a certain time each day. Take advantage of these tools. Screen time should be earned rather than automatically granted to children. Many parents find it helpful to provide kids with a checklist before they are allowed to play video games or watch their favorite shows. Did they spend time reading or practicing their instruments? Are their chores completed for the day? Have they finished their homework and done something creative? Screen time then becomes a relaxing reward rather than a monster that consumes their entire childhood.

All children have interests and gifts, and parents must do their best to encourage those interests that don't involve technology. Does your son or daughter love hiking, kicking a soccer ball, or fishing? Do they love to hear music or to build things out of what they find? A variety of classes and activities can help them pursue those interests for little money. In fact, many local clubs and community colleges offer programs designed specifically to help youngsters develop skills they can continue to build on in the future. This is especially important during the summer months when school is out of session. Encourage them to explore nature or their neighborhood, read books, or play board games with friends and siblings instead. All of these activities can help stimulate our children's creativity while helping them learn things in an organic, natural, and motivational way. As parents, we can be mentors who show our kids how to explore their natural interests. These are the types of hearts that are hard for the devil to gain a foothold in.

It is important to note that the people your children hang out with are pivotal in helping your children discover their strengths and skills. If their friends spend a great deal of time complaining, arguing, or looking for ways that others can serve them, chances are high that these nasty habits will rub off on your children. However, if their peers are naturally curious about life and have a desire to succeed, these good habits will rub off on your kids, as well.

HOW TO TREAT OTHERS

As Christians, it is important that we set limits and expectations for our kids in terms of how they treat other people. They must learn the importance of not taking something that is not theirs. They should understand that lying is never OK. They should respect their parents. They must learn never to mock others.

This last one—not mocking others—holds true whether the person being hurt is present or not. As parents, we should never set examples of gossiping about others or tearing others down behind their backs. Instead our words should be used to inspire, encourage, and build others up.

ESTABLISHING CONSEQUENCES

We know from God's Word that human beings are sinful by nature. Our children do not naturally want to do what is right; if given the choice, many children would rather disobey their parents and do whatever they want. That is why it is critical for parents to have consequences in place and that they implement them whenever children disobey. If we say we are going to give consequences but never follow through, our children will learn to disregard us. It is important that we not just establish rules and expectations but that we also enforce them.

IF WE SAY WE ARE GOING TO GIVE CONSEQUENCES BUT NEVER FOLLOW THROUGH, OUR CHILDREN WILL LEARN TO DISREGARD US.

Every consequence should be consistent with the crime. You should not ground your son for three months for making a rude comment to his sister, for instance. An apology and perhaps helping sister with her chores for the evening might drive the lesson home instead. Larger offenses, such as lying or stealing, should be met with larger consequences, such as grounding or withholding their allowance.

No matter the offense or the consequence, however, it is important for children to understand *why* they are being penalized. These offenses violate *God's laws.* You want your children to be raised with character and integrity, to learn how to live in obedience to the King. Take time to come alongside them and help them understand how their disobedience is not just against you but also against God. Help them see that your discipline is for their good, to help shape them into godly men and women, and that you will continue to instruct and discipline them in love—for their own good!—for as long as they live in your home.

The best consequences are given immediately after your child has disobeyed. You want them to associate the act of doing something wrong with a negative outcome, particularly if they are younger. As discussed previously, it is also important to be consistent. Avoid letting certain offenses go while punishing others; such inconsistency can be confusing for children and may invite further disobedience as they begin to believe you are not really serious about the rules you have in place.

Consequences should also be age appropriate. Time-outs may work for younger children but be ineffective for teens. A more constructive consequence for teens is taking away privileges for a period of time, such as not allowing them to attend a social event or taking away their phone for a week. Consequences like these can be efficacious when it comes to alcohol or drug use. The first time we find out our children have been drinking or getting high, we need to implement consequences immediately—consequences that are painful enough to make our kids think very hard the next time they are tempted to try.

POSITIVE ATTENTION

Remember the 4:1 principle? It bears repeating here. Experts recommend that consequences for poor behavior be accompanied by positive attention for the actions you want to see, and we must always keep this at the forefront of our minds as we implement discipline and correction. This is especially important for sensitive kids who can be devastated by criticism. Make sure you compliment your children for being nice to their siblings or for completing their chores on time. They will want to know that you see them and appreciate their efforts to move in the right direction.

It is also possible to use consequences as uplifting influences in our children's lives. For example, we may want to bake brownies with our kids while they're grounded, showing them that we still enjoy their company even though they have done something wrong. Remember that God is a Father who loves us despite our sin and who wants everyone to come to Him (see 1 Timothy 2:4). Your children should never feel like they have been "written off" because of disobedience. Instead, they should know that although you are hurt and upset, you still forgive them and consider them to be your precious children.

YOUR CHILDREN SHOULD NEVER
FEEL LIKE THEY HAVE BEEN "WRITTEN OFF"
BECAUSE OF DISOBEDIENCE.

RESPECTING DIFFERENCES

If you have ever been to the gym, you know that your body will tell you what its limits are, and you also know that the exercises that are right for someone else to get fit might not be the right exercises for you. This is because there are different body types. Some folks are lean, with long muscles and very little body fat, while others are naturally softer and rounder. Some individuals will need to do more aerobic exercise to stay in shape, while others will require more heavy lifting.

In the same way, our children have a variety of personalities that should inform the way we discipline them. Some kids have strong wills, for example, and tend to resist too much rule setting by parents. While it may be tempting to get into power struggles with these kids, you need to stick to your consequences in a firm, patient tone of voice. Resist the urge to explain yourself too much. If possible, offer choices so that a child like this can feel more in control. For example, you may want to say, "You need to choose a vegetable for dinner. You can have broccoli or asparagus." This will result in a better outcome than if you simply say, "I said to eat your vegetables."

Other children are more sensitive. These kids notice their environments more and process information more thoroughly, and they are also more prone to shutting down or having melt-downs when being disciplined. Sensitive children may require a bit of extra padding when they do something wrong. For example, you could start with a positive comment before launching into your correction, such as, "I know that you're a mature young lady, so I'm surprised that this happened." You can also help them to digest the information by validating their feelings, telling them things like, "I understand why you're frustrated." Sensitive children often simply need to be reassured that they are not monsters or worse than anyone else for having misbehaved. They just need to learn the lesson that these moments are teaching them, and then they can continue developing into the talented individuals they were created to be.

There are also those children who are very free-spirited and fun-loving. These kids may be easy to connect with, since they enjoy spending time with their parents and going on outings. It may be tempting to forgo discipline with this type of child since you do not want to dampen their spirits, but it is important to establish basic consequences when these children step out of line, as well. Just like with all types of children, however, you will want to back up your correction with lots of positive reinforcement and praise for the things they are doing right.

UNDERSTANDING THE BIG PICTURE

No matter the type of child you are correcting and instructing, it is critical to let them know the long-term benefits of your discipline, which is the *"peaceful fruit of righteousness"* that Scripture talks about in Hebrews 12:11. When we obey God's law, the chances of suffering from negative consequences in this life are greatly diminished. We all make mistakes, but living within the parameters of responsible behavior makes life more manageable.

WHEN WE OBEY GOD'S LAW, THE CHANCES OF SUFFERING FROM NEGATIVE CONSEQUENCES IN THIS LIFE ARE GREATLY DIMINISHED. WE ALL MAKE MISTAKES, BUT LIVING WITHIN THE PARAMETERS OF RESPONSIBLE BEHAVIOR MAKES LIFE MORE MANAGEABLE.

Raising a family as a single parent, for example, means that one person will need to work full-time, raise the children, and look after the household. That is an almost impossible burden, and it is a major reason why God is against divorce (see Matthew 5:31–32). He designed marriage as a partnership in which both spouses can help alleviate the work of the other. It is also important, within that partnership, for both parents to be on the same page. They must agree on the standards they will require and the consequences they will be implementing. If young people do not see this model, they will find it very easy to disobey, doing whatever they see fit.

Children who are raised to obey the law of their heavenly Father will be kinder, more honest, and better equipped to meet the demands of life. They will learn to work hard and not have to deal with the underlying fear that comes from breaking the law and trying to get away with it. They can serve the world with their spiritual gifts and enjoy a consistent peace that passes understanding (see Philippians 4:7). Setting the law at home is work—but it is good work that will be rewarding for your entire family for a lifetime.

SIX

ROSE-COLORED GLASSES

In the 1940s, French singer Édith Piaf popularized the song "La vie en rose" throughout the world. The lyrics talk about seeing "life in pink" and about that feeling of exuberance that comes from being in love. We feel all our troubles and sorrows fade into the background when there is a cotton-candy cloud of affection consuming our view and fogging up our better judgment.

There are rose-colored seasons in all our lives, and one of those is when we have children. Parents embrace their honey-blessed babies with great wonder and awe, as is fitting when new life is brought into the world. All children deserve parents who see the best in them. Our offspring may have great potential, and we can envision them becoming great athletes, artists, or experts in some field or other when they grow up.

At the same time, we need to understand that while our children have been kissed by heaven, they are also being chased by hell. The Bible tells us to *"be sober-minded; be watchful. Your adversary the devil prowls around like a roaring lion, seeking someone to devour"* (1 Peter 5:8). In the wild, the youngest prey is eaten first because it is the easiest to carry off. The same holds true in the spiritual realm. Our enemy will not make allowances for our children because they are young. In fact, like a lion in the jungle seeking the easiest prey, Satan will look to use our children's naivete and vulnerability to trap them early—and often he will do it through the poor examples set by parents.

LIKE A LION IN THE JUNGLE SEEKING THE
EASIEST PREY, SATAN WILL LOOK TO USE OUR
CHILDREN'S NAIVETE AND VULNERABILITY TO
TRAP THEM EARLY.

Children are more sensitive and attuned to our behaviors than we realize. They are watching us more than they are listening to us. It is our job to stop pretending that everything is perfect and sweet. We need to see our children for who they are, realistically evaluate our own parenting, and acknowledge how our choices are impacting our kids.

THE RIGHT KIND OF ACTIVITY

If you have ever been to a school soccer field on the weekends, you know what the culture is like. Many parents are friendly, but their anxious eyes are constantly scanning the field, wondering if their child is scoring as many goals as their peers. Parents will cheer for those athletes who make good plays and berate the ones who don't, without much regard for the fact that the players are just kids trying to enjoy a sport. The truth is that, in those six or seven soccer fields full of little kickers, only one or two players will end up playing at higher levels. Many of them are pressured by the unrealistic expectations of their parents. Sports are great for helping youngsters make friends and become part of a community, but they were never meant to prove a person's worth to the world.

Some kids thrive on being pushed. These young people hear a harsh word and rise to the challenge. They long for competition and stubbornly commit to being the best no matter what. We should never seek to quench that drive. There are also plenty of young people, however, who would be devastated by that type of critical feedback. Some kids need a kind word of encouragement more than overly zealous pushing, and we would be better off helping them overcome their shyness and sense of inadequacy than forcing them to perform.

Our desire to have the best player in the world living in our home must take a backseat to our child's needs. We must take an honest look at our kids and what they require in terms of nurturing. What are their real strengths and desires? What kinds of things are they always happy doing? How can we see life through their eyes? You may be surprised at what you learn through an honest conversation. Your child may have talents and secret goals that never even occurred to you.

The same holds true in the classroom. Some kids are natural students who will soak up everything their teachers say. Most youngsters, however, have hurdles to overcome. They will excel in some classes but struggle in others. This is often due to their particular learning style. Visual learners, for example, retain knowledge best if they can see it. They may need to write down what they hear in class in order to remember it or organize information on charts or index cards to study for a test. Auditory learners retain information by listening, and they often remember material best if they can talk about it with someone else; class participation and study groups are helpful for these types of learners.

You may also have a student who is a kinesthetic learner. These folks are at their finest when working with their hands. They may be natural athletes or mechanics. These students learn best by being physically active while trying to retain information, whether that means fiddling with a stress ball or even walking. Finally, some children are reading and writing learners. These youngsters need to read and rephrase information—either in their heads or on paper—to ensure they understand it. Students who learn best this way need to constantly take notes while reading or sitting in class so that they absorb what they read and hear.[9]

We need to understand that every child learns differently, and it is our job as parents to accept the reality of who our kids are and make adjustments along the way, depending upon their strengths and weaknesses, as we prepare them for school and life. When it comes to academics, we must accept that if our child does not learn something the minute he reads it, that does not mean he is without abilities. In terms of athletics, we can accept that our youngster may not be the next Simone Biles or David Beckham. Our children are uniquely beautiful, perfectly designed by God, with talents different from those of anyone else. Our children might excel where we did not think they would while also struggling where we thought they would be strong. We must never shame our children for who they are but rather embrace the children God has gifted to us. Each child has been knit together, with a specific purpose ordained by our heavenly Father (see Psalm 139:13).

OUR CHILDREN ARE UNIQUELY BEAUTIFUL, PERFECTLY DESIGNED BY GOD, WITH TALENTS DIFFERENT FROM THOSE OF ANYONE ELSE.

Many parents dream of their child throwing that ninety mile per hour fastball in ninth grade, but we have also heard stories about top athletes who sustained single injuries that ended their athletic careers before they even started college. Your child should be active, but that activity should be balanced. Even if they are gifted in sports, that time on the field or in the gym should be complemented by time in church and with friends.

---

9. For more information about these various learning styles identified by Peter Fleming, please refer to I. J. Prithishkumar and S. A. Michael, "Understanding Your Student: Using the VARK Model," *J Postgrad Med* 60, no. 2: (Apr–Jun 2014): 183-6, https://pubmed.ncbi.nlm.nih.gov/24823519/.

For many kids, their giftings might not be in athletics or academics; it might be church activity or creative works to which God has called them instead. He might have a different kind of game in mind for your kid than you do! Remember, being a servant does not require exceptional intelligence or athletic ability. We need only the will to serve. Children must learn to work hard, but they should do it all for the glory of God (see 1 Corinthians 10:31).

Unconditional love means showing our children that we love them even if they are not star athletes or valedictorians. We still want to go for walks with them, take them to the beach, and just spend time getting to know them. Many young people are crushed when they realize they have not met their parents' expectations. We must show our children that we love them no matter what, in the same way the Father does, and that as long as they are on this earth, there is an important purpose for their lives.

MULTIPLE INTELLIGENCES

We often push our children into categories and give them labels, such as "jock" or "smart," but we must remember there are many intelligence types and that individuals are skilled in different ways. These various aptitudes can blossom into wonderful contributions to the world if we can detect and cultivate them in our children. We must allow their natural gifts to develop and ought to provide healthy outlets for what they want to do. Pushing in other areas will result only in resentment and frustration for both you and your child.

Howard Gardner is an American developmental psychologist who graduated from Harvard in 1965. He is best known for his theory of multiple intelligences, which suggests that intelligence manifests itself in a variety of ways. Children who do not excel in traditional areas like reading, writing, and arithmetic still have unique types of "smarts" that they can refine and use to make the world a better place.[10]

CHILDREN WHO DO NOT EXCEL IN TRADITIONAL AREAS LIKE READING, WRITING, AND ARITHMETIC STILL HAVE UNIQUE TYPES OF "SMARTS" THAT THEY CAN REFINE AND USE TO MAKE THE WORLD A BETTER PLACE.

Young people with good visual and spatial intelligence, for example, are adept at seeing the whole picture. They love to analyze maps, charts, and graphs. These kiddos may seem disorganized at first, but they are quite good at coming up with outside-of-the-box solutions to problems. They may love playing with building blocks or puzzles and enjoy painting or the performing arts. Such individuals are the architects, interior designers, and engineers of tomorrow. If your child demonstrates these types of talents, you can hone these skills through drawing lessons, design classes, or instruction in computer programming.

Those with linguistic or verbal intelligence are our readers and writers. When you give these children unscheduled time, usually they will spend it with their noses in books. Such children can give clear explanations and love to tell stories. They are the writers, teachers, and politicians of tomorrow. If you recognize signs of linguistic intelligence in your child, cultivating this gift may mean ordering books regularly, especially during school breaks! You may also want to sign your son or daughter up for creative writing classes.

---

10. For more information about Howard Gardner's theory of multiple intelligences, please see Hani Morgan, "Howard Gardner's Multiple Intelligences Theory and His Ideas on Promoting Creativity," in *Celebrating Giants and Trailblazers: A-Z of Who's Who in Creativity Research and Related Fields*, ed. Fredricka Reisman, 124–141 (London, UK: KIE Publications, 2021), https://aquila.usm.edu/fac_pubs/19828/.

Other children are much more factual, and these are the ones with logical and mathematical intelligence. They love to analyze numbers and solve computations. Your child's teachers may tell you that your child has an aptitude for math and is great at problem-solving. Auditors, accountants, and statisticians are all folks who have wonderful logical skills.

Of course, not all children fit into traditional academic molds. Youngsters skilled with movement and sports may have bodily/kinesthetic intelligence. These kiddos are easy to pick out, as they are naturals on the field or in the dance studio. They can pick up baseball bats and get right into the mix with their peers, hitting line drives in no time, or sashay through ballet classes, demonstrating natural flexibility, strength, and grace. Signing your kid up for a team or classes is the obvious thing to do, but you might also encourage him or her to consider a future as a builder, a physical trainer, or a craftsperson. The school years provide wonderful opportunities for these kinesthetic kids to get active and figure out which types of movement they enjoy the most and are skilled in.

You may also have a child with musical intelligence. These young performers find it easiest to remember information when it is set to music. They might easily pick up an instrument and learn how to play it, or they will remember every melody they have heard. Children with musical intelligence can develop a lot of skills through instrument lessons and by participating in musicals and concerts.

Gardner also recognized interpersonal skills as an important type of intelligence. Individuals with strong interpersonal skills may listen carefully to their friends' problems and be able to empathize easily with different emotions and perspectives. These individuals are well-liked by their peers because of their willingness to understand and uplift others. They are good friends, and within the church, these are the folks who are quick to reach out to those in need with the love and care of Christ. In terms of careers, these individuals are often best suited to counseling or psychology. They can also play important roles in the church, serving as small group leaders or Sunday school teachers.

Some individuals also have good knowledge and understanding of themselves, which Gardner called "intrapersonal intelligence." These folks are keenly aware of their own strengths and weaknesses and can analyze their own thoughts and feelings. These are our writers and philosophers. Within the church, these men and women may serve as a kind of conscience, showing others how to hold themselves to a higher standard of righteousness as believers.

Finally, some people may demonstrate naturalist intelligence. My son falls into this category. He loves to hike and explore the great outdoors, easily identifying creatures and species. God has designed these individuals to love and respect His creation while imparting this knowledge to others. These individuals make great conservationists and park specialists, and, as they help others see the beauty of creation, they can point to the beauty and glory of the Creator Himself!

Observant parents know how to recognize the signs of different types of intelligence in their children. You may, for example, always see your daughter plunking at the piano (musical intelligence) or notice how much your son always asks to go camping (naturalist intelligence). The child always weaving creative stories has probably been wired with high linguistic intelligence, while the child who is a compassionate friend probably scores high in interpersonal intelligence. In addition to observation, you might consider tests that children can take to help identify their natural strengths.

OBSERVANT PARENTS KNOW HOW TO
RECOGNIZE THE SIGNS OF DIFFERENT TYPES OF
INTELLIGENCE IN THEIR CHILDREN.

As a parent and as someone who works with youth, I have found the best way to reach children is to ask them what they enjoy doing and then encourage them to do that with their whole hearts. This does not mean that we put our rose-colored glasses back on and pretend our youngsters are the best in the world at everything. It simply means that we recognize how they are skilled and that we let them know we love them as they pursue those endeavors, no matter what.

A WORD TO CHURCH LEADERS

It is a sad truth that those in church leadership, including pastors, are often the parents of children who struggle the most. These young people may notice hypocrisy both in their families and within their churches, and the devil has his eye on them due to their prominence when it comes to outsiders looking in at the church community. As parents, especially those who are in church leadership, we must be very careful about the types of examples we set. Are we arguing with our spouses or harping on each other's flaws? Are we complaining about church activities when no one is around? Our children will see this and wonder if our faith is genuine. Our lives must teach them that God is real and that life is worth living well.

WE MUST NURTURE AND CARE FOR OUR
CHILDREN AS THEY ARE, NOT AS WE IMAGINE
THEM TO BE IN OUR PINK AND PERFECT WORLDS.

None of us is perfect, but we still must strive to do what the Bible calls us to do, and with respect to our children, we need to take off our rose-colored glasses. Look at them honestly. Take stock of their positive *and* negative traits. Do they seem to be angry? Are they unaffected by the things of the Lord? Are they sitting ducks for bad decisions?

We must nurture and care for our children as they are, not as we imagine them to be in our pink and perfect worlds. They are people with unique struggles, gifts, and challenges. Our children require conversations, listening, and leadership. They must see consistent love and abiding patience in us. They must know that we respect their special makeup of gifts and abilities. And they should see us take off our hazy goggles, willing to accept them for the young men and women God is building up rather than the fulfillment of our own dreams. The reality may be even better than what you had planned.

PART TWO: RECOVERY

All the work I do in my ministry is in recovery. This section, slightly longer than the previous, will deal with this vital but difficult work. While you may not share my calling to help hundreds of young people recover from addictions, you may very well have an addict in your life whom you long to see set free from the chains of addiction that bind them. My prayers are with you, and all that I know about this process I will share with you now in Part Two.

SEVEN

THE HIDDEN TEAR

The home should be a haven, but when the home that is supposed to be stress reducing becomes stress producing, then holes form in the fabric of a child's soul. Most of these holes, these tears, stay hidden for a long time until they manifest in emotional problems that lead to certain behaviors. In these environments, little by little, our kids are torn apart. What is desperately needed is to expose what is hidden, to uncover these tears. Until we understand that something is hurting them, we will not be able to get our kids the help they need.

STORYTELLING SCARS

It's said that a picture is worth a thousand words. I think the same holds true for scars. Scars tell stories. Did you know that a scar is stronger than the skin around it? Scars produce strength and character, but that doesn't mean we should ignore scars or accept all scars as inherently good. To understand healing is one thing, but to understand how the scar got there in the first place is another thing entirely. We must ask questions like, "What happened?" and "How did it get there in the first place?" Only then can healing begin.

The typical person has multiple storytelling scars, and when it comes to our young people, we must help them make sense of these scars. Who can help them with their scars and tears? Which parents, grandparents, or other guardians have the wisdom and compassion to understand them and then help them? Who is healing them and building them up? Who can see what is hidden? We must prepare them to receive help as we nurture and care for them.

THE TYPICAL PERSON HAS MULTIPLE
STORYTELLING SCARS, AND WHEN IT COMES TO
OUR YOUNG PEOPLE, WE MUST HELP THEM MAKE
SENSE OF THESE SCARS.

It's OK to be scarred. We all are. Consider the biggest, baddest lions in the jungle. No one gets to be king of the jungle without a face and body full of scars. Where there are no scars, there have been no fights. Where there are no fights, there are no humbling losses or triumphant victories. We must prepare our kids from a very early age for the battles they will face in life. They must know it is normal to have scars and realize that those scars, if understood properly, can be good things.

HIDDEN HURTS

Some scars run so deep that we don't see them. Can you see a scar on the heart? Sometimes the heart is being torn apart day by day, but we fail to see it—or we don't want to. Sooner or later, the tearing of a young heart can't be ignored. As time goes on, the spiritual tear in a young person's heart will extend deeper and deeper, and if it's not addressed, it will begin to scar on its own. It becomes calloused and calcified, leading to a "hardening of the heart." These are the scars we don't want. These are the scars that crush our kids, ruling them. These are the scars that, if not discovered and mended, lead to destructive paths. The hardening of a young person's heart is simply the natural outcome of ignored, hidden hurt.

SOMETIMES THE HEART IS BEING TORN APART DAY BY DAY, BUT WE FAIL TO SEE IT—OR WE DON'T WANT TO.

Are we training our kids to fear pain and hurt? We need to let our kids understand it's OK and normal to get hurt. When they fall on the playground, let them take care of themselves instead of running to check on them at their every stumble. They need to know that getting hurt is a normal part of life in this fallen world. As they grow and mature, they won't get hurt just physically but spiritually and emotionally, too. If we can address this forthrightly, helping them to understand that pain is normal and can be discussed, the tears won't be hidden. The scarring won't be deep but will rather remain on the surface, where it can strengthen them.

Where we have missed hurts, however, and where hurts have plunged deep and torn the soul, we need to do whatever we can to address them. These are the hidden tears that can rip our kids apart and lead to hardened hearts. Most people see only the outside and say things like, "You look fantastic! Everything is going so well for you!" But the appearance rarely matches reality, and when you find that out, it may be too late. We must address these hidden hurts as soon as possible, as soon as we suspect them.

BEING THE LIFELINE

With my son's traumatic brain injury, you can't see the scars on his brain. You can see the effects of his brain injury, but the scars themselves are hidden. You can clearly see the changed life brought about by a brain injury, but the scar—the tear itself—is hidden. In the same way, you can see the scar on his throat where they performed a tracheotomy. That scar tells a story—when someone has that kind of scar, you know they were on a breathing machine, fighting for their life.

Sometimes *we* need to be the ones helping our children breathe. Like the machine that kept my son alive, we need to be lifelines for our kids. They need to understand it's OK to come to us for fresh air, whether that's encouragement and positive words or quality time together. We want them to realize they can rely on us for life-giving support twenty-four seven.

SOMETIMES *WE* NEED TO BE THE ONES HELPING
OUR CHILDREN BREATHE. LIKE THE MACHINE
THAT KEPT MY SON ALIVE, WE NEED TO BE
LIFELINES FOR OUR KIDS.

Some parents are so strict that they are anything but a breath of fresh air for their kids. They are so adamant and unyielding about their beliefs that they hurt their children more than help them. Sadly, that was how I parented in many seasons of my life. I was so "heavenly-minded" that I was of no earthly good. I wanted the best for my children—I still do—but often, instead of presenting the gospel, I just gave them rules. Rather than listening to them to help uncover their hidden tears, especially in middle school and high school, I just focused on outward appearances and assumed they were doing well. Their tears were hidden, and so the hurt beneath the surface was compounded. I didn't understand at this point the kind of balance needed between correction and edification, or the importance of regular, intentional encouragement.

We parents must understand that we are part of the reason for those tears—and we need to know we can be part of the healing, too. We must first accept that we have done some damage. Everyone does. It is an ongoing process for our kids to become stronger, and we have to stay engaged the whole way. This is never easy, and it can be even more difficult in single-parent homes and in blended families. In these cases, parents are usually trying to heal their own wounds, as well, which makes it even more difficult for them to help heal their kids. The work is always worth it, however, and our kids deserve our help in this healing process.

FACING YOUR OWN HURTS AND SCARS

Consider this: So much of who we are has been inherited from our fathers and from their fathers, so helping our kids starts with figuring out some of our own stuff first. You need to find *your* hidden tears, pulling back layers until you expose the hurt, and then begin the hard work of your own healing. Who likes to do that? Almost no one. It requires hard work and moments of major discomfort. Yet it is worth it, for our own sakes as well as our kids'.

Get down to that very bottom scar. Pray and ask God to show you where your deepest hurt lies. Then take it to Christ. "Here it is!" you can say to Him. "Here are some of the issues in my life. Here is where I'm hurt. Can You please mend it and make it better?"

We know that if we do that, He will heal us. But just as Christ rose from the dead with scars in His hands, feet, and side (see John 20:27), so too will we carry these scars all our days. We will be healed, but we will remember what we've gone through, the things He has healed in us. We can't get around pain, but Christ in us can redeem the past, the present, and the future. In Jesus we can make new stories—glory stories.

WE CAN'T GET AROUND PAIN, BUT CHRIST IN US
CAN REDEEM THE PAST, THE PRESENT,
AND THE FUTURE. IN JESUS WE CAN MAKE NEW
STORIES—GLORY STORIES.

Once we begin to understand the hidden tear—exposing it little by little, changing the bandage, reapplying the medicine—it will begin to heal. Practically, it looks like this: You admit you are hurt. You look at that wound, you face it, and you give it to God to begin healing. Until you are completely healed, you keep checking it every day, applying the medicine and changing out the bandage.

What is the medicine? The truth of the gospel. God loves you. He sent His one and only Son to die for you so that you could be with Him now and forever. He has forgiven your every sin, your every stupid choice and shameful mistake. He has come to you so that you may have life to the full, including healing and wholeness.

HOW HE HEALS

All things are possible with God. In His mercy and goodness, He heals not only our hidden tears but also those of our children. Practically speaking, what does this process look like? It starts with understanding each child individually. We cannot continue to slap the scar, trying to make it thicker, while ignoring the tear underneath. We must ask questions like, "Why are they like this? Who is helping them? Who is encouraging them? Who is setting them up to fail? Who is setting them up to succeed?" We play vital roles as parents and as adults in their lives when it comes to helping them make good choices. We can't force them to make the right choices, but we can present the choices to them and help them think through the best path.

When a person gets an X-ray, that image shows the bones inside. When a person gets an MRI, it shows an even more detailed image. The trained eyes of a doctor can then look at those images and determine how bad an injury is. As parents, we often fail to seek out the doctor to help us understand the tear and how bad it is. We hesitate to ask for help.

It is important for parents to get with other parents for support when there is a problem. If we will cast our burdens on the Lord, He promises to sustain us and not let us slip (see Psalm

121:3). He will never leave or forsake us (see Hebrews 13:5). He will establish our plans (Proverbs 16:3). As parents, we need those who will care for us and nurture us along the way. That is part of how the Lord sustains us and cares for us. Having just one or two good, godly friends going through the same things we are can be so encouraging, uplifting, and helpful.

TIPS FOR HELPING

When we are trying to help others—whether we are helping a fellow parent or trying to help our own children—some of the most damaging things we can say are, "You *should* do this," or "You *shouldn't* do that." So many of our hidden tears are based on unrealized shoulds and shouldn'ts. We "help" our kids this way at their own peril.

How many of us have uttered, "You should be more like your sister," or "Your brother never acted that way"? Each of us essentially bears God's fingerprints, showing how He has uniquely woven us together. We each have different colored eyes, hair, and skin, and we are exactly the way God wants us. He has given us unique strengths—including the strength to stand firm amid the pain of our hidden tears. We must understand this, though: The reason many good kids "go bad" is because their hurts are so deep.

When a woman gives birth by C-section, a scar is left behind. If she has another baby, her medical team will usually recut that original scar and deliver her next baby through it. That scar is beneficial because it is easier to cut that scar again than to make a new scar, going deep again to get out that beautiful life that is there inside the mother. In the same way, it can be painful for us to reopen scars, but it is worth it as we go deep to bring out new life. The new scar, although still a scar, can heal up even stronger than before.

IT CAN BE PAINFUL FOR US TO REOPEN SCARS,
BUT IT IS WORTH IT AS WE GO DEEP TO BRING
OUT NEW LIFE.

DEALING WITH FEAR, RESENTMENT, AND HATRED

Trapped underneath the surface of what looks like a healed outward scar, one often finds fear, resentment, and hatred. Going beneath the surface is bloody. It's messy. Opening up an old wound to clean out what's inside takes commitment. Just as medical surgery is not for the faint of heart, so healing hidden emotional tears takes courage. There is a lot of pain involved with this process, but in the end, it is better than having an infection, a festering tear on the inside.

It is not weak to face your pain—but it does hurt. Young people often turn to drugs and alcohol because that pain is too great. That's when they start making truly bad decisions, when many will simply deem themselves "bad kids." How did that good kid go so bad? It is the hidden tears, the scars in his or her life. This is when we need to come around our young people, understand them better, give them credit where credit is due, and even be a little harder when necessary.

Consider a young person who frequently lies and manipulates people. This person is trying to please others and has no room to cultivate truth, but, ultimately, truth is the only thing that can bring healing. It is truth that will heal each person of the scars and hidden tears under the surface. When we understand the truth, we must bring it up gently and lovingly. We must demonstrate it more with our actions than with our words. We must share it in a way that will be accepted.

Unfortunately, when good kids go bad, it is very difficult for them to accept the truth. Deep down they know it is what they need, but because their scars have become so hardened, they resist being strengthened through the truth. This is when we need to see young people differently and bring compassion to the table. I have heard parents say—in front of their kids—that the choices their kids are making are tearing them apart. What do you suppose that kind of a comment does to a kid who overhears it?

Everyone has hidden tears—everyone. Sadly, sometimes the worst tears are in the kids of pastors and those raised in good homes. These kids hear all the time how they are supposed to be good, but what they see from their parents is sometimes a different story. This is where the worst tears come from.

No matter what caused the hidden tears, we must seek to understand them. We must not judge our kids but rather listen to them with compassion, and then—expertly, surgically, and lovingly—apply the truth, humbly acknowledging our complicity in causing the deep tears in their hearts, as we endeavor to bring them to the Great Physician who can heal them.

EIGHT

HIDDEN TREASURE
BENEATH SKELETONS

Picture a shipwreck. A pirate ship has run aground. Hundreds of years later, someone discovers the wreckage. Two things they would be likely to find, at least in a storybook about this type of thing, are skeletons and sunken treasure. First, picture a skeleton and what it represents—death and things that have decayed. Now, think about treasure—a chest of gold and jewels, for example. It isn't dead, for it was never alive. And the coins will not have lost their value. To me, treasures represent life, and they are sought after because they are worth something. People dream of obtaining treasures because treasures can be powerful tools in changing lives for the better.

Every single person has treasure within them, placed there by our Creator who has fearfully and wonderfully knit us together. God can powerfully use these treasures to build His kingdom as others see the treasure of salvation in our lives and long for what we have. These treasures, however, are often buried beneath piles of skeletons, like a chest in a wrecked pirate ship.

THE SKELETONS IN OUR LIVES

We all have skeletons in our lives. These are the unhealthy attitudes, thoughts, and habits that don't encourage thriving but instead drag us down and can lead toward death. These might be actions, habits, or even unhelpful ways of thinking. Sometimes we are even living alongside someone else's skeletons without knowing it; kids rarely realize when they are coexisting with skeletons from their parents' own upbringing.

The more skeletons there are, the more deeply buried the treasure might be under rotting bones; and the deeper the treasure lies in that pile, the harder it will be to find. The important thing we must realize, however, is that the treasure is always there— somewhere. Every single young person you meet is valuable, full of treasure.

THE TREASURE IS ALWAYS THERE—SOMEWHERE.
EVERY SINGLE YOUNG PERSON YOU MEET IS
VALUABLE, FULL OF TREASURE.

The question we've been trying to answer in this book is, "Why do good kids go bad?" This book is a diagnostic investigation, a desperate attempt to understand the tragedy of unrealized potential, especially a potential stolen by "going bad"—that is, by giving one's life over to substance abuse, which piles on more and more skeletons until the treasure is so far buried that it might as well not even be there. When my brother and millions of others like him died before reaching their God-given potential, that is exactly what happened: they died with buried treasure, undiscovered, unutilized, unrealized. It's tragic.

These skeletons keep people down as they keep their treasures buried. When loved ones die, those are skeletons. When friends betray us, those are skeletons. When parents fall short, those are skeletons. Skeletons are unavoidable in life. Even the best among us have fallen short and helped to heap up skeletons, on ourselves and others. There is no perfect parent, no perfect home. Some homes are certainly less healthy than others, but everyone—and

I mean *everyone*—has skeletons from their home life and upbringing. Detriment has been handed down from generation to generation, from one society to another—piles and piles of personal and cultural skeletons—covering up incredibly beautiful, multifaceted treasures.

DETRIMENT HAS BEEN HANDED DOWN FROM
GENERATION TO GENERATION, FROM ONE
SOCIETY TO ANOTHER—PILES AND PILES OF
PERSONAL AND CULTURAL SKELETONS—
COVERING UP INCREDIBLY BEAUTIFUL,
MULTIFACETED TREASURES.

SKELETONS BROUGHT TO LIFE

When archeologists discover long-buried bones, they understand something important: They are at the beginning of a story, opening to the first pages of a new book, and the bones they unearth will be the "words" that tell that story. In a sense, the skeletons they have found are like treasures themselves.

How do we see our own metaphorical skeletons? Do we realize that God can turn these dead things into treasures of life? Think about the times in Scripture when God brought skeletons back to life. Lazarus, for instance, had been dead four days when Jesus called out to him in a loud voice, "*Lazarus, come out*" (John 11:43). Lazarus had already been wrapped in burial cloth and was well on his way to decay; a skeleton would be all that was left of Lazarus once enough time had passed. Jesus, however, commanded him to come forth; He called forth treasure from skeleton, life from death. It was a miracle when Lazarus came out of the grave, restored to life, and it was a miracle when Jesus told those around Lazarus to unbind him and let him go.

Did you know that, because of Christ's work on the cross and the Holy Spirit living in us, *we* can take part in this same kind of "unbinding" miracle? Just as Jesus told Lazarus's friends to unbind him, He calls us to help unbind those around us. When God restores a skeleton—that is, when He brings that which is spiritually dead to life—then we who are around that person must see ourselves like those who were near Lazarus on that day. We must hear Christ say to us, "*Unbind him, and let him go*" (John 11:44).

It is Christ who brings us to life, and then we have the great privilege of being there to walk with each other in this new life and help "unbind" the past burdens that entangle us. I take this to mean that we are called to *help* those in our lives—never to force or control them. We must nurture others, care for them, and understand that there is treasure down deep. As parents and guardians, we need to be excavators on a mission to unearth those buried treasures.

WHY DO WE HAVE SKELETONS?

James 1:17 tells us, "*Every good gift and every perfect gift is from above, coming down from the Father of lights.*" All good things are from God, but what about the bad things, the negative things? Where did all these skeletons come from? I'll tell you: They come from the pit of hell.

According to Ephesians 6:12, "*We do not wrestle against flesh and blood, but against the rulers, against the authorities, against the cosmic powers over this present darkness, against the spiritual forces of evil in the heavenly places.*" Notice that we fight against "*authorities,*" plural. In the King James Version, this word is translated as "*principalities.*" A principality is technically a state ruled by a prince. There are states of darkness overlorded by demonic rulers, and they throw garbage at us all the time. There is an old saying that everyone has skeletons in the closet. I believe that! I also believe that if you drag those bones out of the closet and into the light, they will tell you a story. They will help you understand your past and give you strength to carry on—but only if you accept them and talk about them. We must be willing to ask ourselves questions. What are our skeletons? How have they hurt us? Will we choose to learn from them? Or will we just let them consume us and take away our time?

VALUING OUR TIME

I want to pause here to talk about time, because time is a precious commodity. Remember the 1,440 principle: Each person has just 1,440 minutes in a day. How are we using that time? Are we wasting it on worries and fruitlessness? Are we heaping up more skeletons and spending all our days consumed by them? Or are we investing our time in good things—in removing the skeletons and unearthing the treasures in our own and others' lives? How many minutes are you willing to give someone that you will never get back? Are you willing to give your time for the sake of another?

The treasures beneath our skeletons are priceless. We have been bought with a high price—the precious blood of Jesus Christ—and we were bought for a specific purpose: to bring out the treasures embedded in us so that we can shine for His glory. Some of those precious minutes in our days must be used for unearthing treasures—for digging up old skeletons, finding buried treasures, and shining them up.

We all know gold is valuable. Why is it valuable? One reason is because it is so rare, much of it buried deep in the ground. Furthermore, gold must go through a refining process, which takes time and energy. It gets heated up so that impurities can be removed, and then it is molded into a finished product, ready to be used.

This is an apt metaphor for the treasures lying in the hearts of young people. Those hidden treasures need to be dug up, refined, polished, and then put to use. When a person grows older, those treasures become even more valuable and appreciated. Young people often cannot see the value of the treasures within them, so they don't take care of their treasures. They don't refine them or polish them but just leave them buried in the ground. Our job is to come alongside them, help them see the value of their treasures, and then help them dig them up.

VALUING THE TREASURE

Have you ever seen a child who's been given more toys than there are at the toy store, or a kid with more pairs of shoes than hairs on his head?

I was an assistant basketball coach for six years at a big high school. My primary job was to coach the players in their strength conditioning. I had no real understanding of the X's and O's, and I didn't know anything about making a game plan. I was just the encourager.

There was a young man named Ian on the team, and he was not a great player. He was clumsy, and we couldn't tell if he was right-handed or left-handed. Maybe he had two left hands! Well, the head coach couldn't cut Ian, because Ian had heart. He showed up to every practice, every open gym. He was a little backward in his personality, but no one worked harder. When the team ran suicides—brutal high-intensity cardio drills—Ian would run so hard that his feet would bleed. Finally the coach figured out Ian's shoes were too small, so he went out and bought Ian a pair of shoes that fit, paying for them out of his own pocket.

The next day Ian came out of the locker room for practice wearing his old shoes.

"Ian, where are your new shoes?" we asked.

"I didn't want to ruin them," he said.

Ian *treasured* his new pair of shoes. Those other kids with pairs and pairs of shoes all over the place couldn't possibly understand that, but Ian got it. He saw the value of those new shoes, so he treasured them.

Treasures aren't properly valued, though, if we don't use them. Remember what I said earlier—that many kids don't recognize their treasures, so they leave them buried? The treasure is meant to be *unearthed* and *used*. The coach told Ian to get back in the locker room and put on his new shoes. Ian was going to *use* that treasure!

TREASURE IS MEANT TO BE *UNEARTHED* AND *USED*.

Ian never was very good at basketball, but on the last game of his senior year, the coach put him in. He got fouled, and when he made one of his shots, the whole team—the whole room, in fact!— went berserk cheering for him. Just as Ian received a *treasure* in those shoes, the coach recognized an even greater treasure—Ian's heart—beneath the bloody feet. The coach saw Ian's treasure and gave him a chance. It turns out Ian was terrible at basketball, but he was incredibly intelligent. (He could read a 700-page book in a weekend!) Ian went on to discover more of his treasure and eventually became an architectural engineer and an expert in horticulture. The coach had brought out the best in Ian—not basketball skills but the treasures of grit and heart.

STOPPING THE SKELETON FACTORIES

Those of us with kids in our lives, especially kids struggling with addictions, must relentlessly remind ourselves that our job, when it comes to these kids, is to see their hidden treasures and to help dig them up. We are here to remove those skeletons—sometimes removing and reburying them elsewhere, and sometimes just exposing them and leaving them in the sun to blanch benignly like a bone left out in the woods. It's still a bone, a symbol of death—but it will eventually become brittle and decompose. That's what needs to happen with these bones piled on top of our kids' treasures. We need to help remove them so that our kids can get free and let their lights shine.

When a kid has a drug or alcohol problem, they have made some poor choices. We need to help them see the skeletons they are creating with those choices. It is death they are creating, and there is always a reason why—we just need to help them figure it out. Why are they doing it? To them, drugs and alcohol are the treasure, making them feel good; but what they think is treasure is actually a curse. What they think is life is actually death. We need to help our kids see that their choices are heaping up new skeletons—and then come alongside and help them stop producing those skeletons.

THE RACE FOR BURIED TREASURE

Have you ever watched a movie about a search for buried treasure? It's a typical backstory: Somebody buried a treasure and left an old, tattered map, and multiple people are fighting to be the first to find it and dig it up. We need to understand that God has a map for each person's life from a very young age. As parents, we need to ask Him to show us His maps for our children's lives, so that we can help them on the paths to their treasures. Then, when they are old, they will not go astray but will cherish and use their treasures for God's glory.

We also must understand that, just as many people seek the buried treasure in the movie, so too do others seek the treasures in our children's hearts. Hell itself is seeking those treasures, and Satan himself will try to steal and destroy the treasures in our children's hearts.

When someone finds a treasure, someone else will always come along and try to take it. That's what a thief does. That's what the liar, the accuser, does. The Bible talks about the deceiver who is coming after you. How many times have we heard that the devil prowls about like a roaring lion, seeking someone to devour? (See 1 Peter 5:8.) He comes for the treasures of your heart, for the treasures of our children's hearts. Out of the abundance of the heart, the mouth flows (see Matthew 12:34). The book of Proverbs tells us to watch over our hearts with all diligence, for from them flow the springs of life (see Proverbs 4:23). There is a treasure in the heart of every person, and it lies beneath the skeletons of life.

WHEN SKELETONS BECOME TREASURES

As we dig, we should not disregard the skeletons that have to be removed. But here's an amazing thing: Sometimes the skeleton itself *becomes* the treasure. Just as our scars tell stories, so do the skeletons in our lives become part of God's unique fingerprint on each of us.

Think of a hunter who has scored a six-point buck. What does he do with the Head? He takes it to a taxidermist and has it stuffed and mounted, a trophy that he will hang proudly on his wall. People see it and admire the big spread. For this trophy to hang on the wall, though, the deer had to die. Any animal on a wall once had life. Now it is a trophy, and it tells a story that lives on.

That skeleton on the wall—whether from a deer or some other big animal—was put there by a taxidermist. Someone caught or killed that game, and then another person took over, one who was gifted with the talent to bring forth—in a way, to resurrect—that animal. The analogy isn't perfect, because the deer is still dead, but it points us to a great truth: *Jesus brings life from death.* He gives life, and He give it abundantly, from the inside out.

JESUS BRINGS LIFE FROM DEATH. HE GIVES LIFE, AND
HE GIVE IT ABUNDANTLY, FROM THE INSIDE OUT.

In the Old Testament, God showed the prophet Ezekiel a valley filled with dry bones:

> The hand of the LORD was upon me, and he brought me out in the Spirit of the LORD and set me down in the middle of the valley; it was full of bones. And he led me around among them, and behold, there were very many on the surface of the valley, and behold, they were very dry. And he said to me, "Son of man, can these bones live?" And I answered, "O Lord GOD, you know." (Ezekiel 37:1–3)

This was one big pile of skeletons—a whole valley, in fact, filled with dead, dry bones. These bones wouldn't stay dead, however. God had plans for those bones. God said to Ezekiel:

> Prophesy over these bones, and say to them, O dry bones, hear the word of the LORD. Thus says the Lord GOD to these bones: Behold, I will cause breath to enter you, and you shall live. And I will lay sinews upon you, and will cause flesh to come upon you, and cover you with skin, and put breath in you, and you shall live, and you shall know that I am the LORD. (Ezekiel 37:4–6)

God's plan was to bring those bones—those dead, dry skeletons—to life! Real life. Not just mounted-deer-head-on-the-wall kind of life, but abundant life, with sinews and flesh and skin and breath. Later in that same passage, God told Israel, through Ezekiel:

> Behold, I will open your graves and raise you from your graves, O my people. And I will bring you into the land of Israel. And you shall know that I am the LORD, when I open your graves, and raise you from your graves, O my people. And I will put

my Spirit within you, and you shall live, and I will place you
in your own land. Then you shall know that I am the LORD; I
have spoken, and I will do it, declares the LORD.

(Ezekiel 37:12–14)

Do you see what happened here? The Lord gave life to those bones and then gave those bones a supreme treasure—His very own Spirit! This is the greatest rags-to-riches story, the saga of spiritually dead men and women being brought from death into life.

Even for those who have been brought into life, however, some of the "old man"—that is, our past skeletons—can still hang on. We still struggle with our own sin nature, and this might include addictions. In the same way that the Lord has resurrected us from death to life, however, He will continue to move out the remaining dead stuff. He is in the business of pulling aside piles of skeletons so that treasures can be revealed, and He will continue to do so for His own glory and for our good (see Romans 8:28).

FROM "GORY" TO "GLORY STORY"

Our past can become a glory story. As the Lord brings dead things to life, His beauty shines. And as He continues to polish the great gifts and treasures that He's placed in us, He is glorified. This is what the sanctification process is all about. Sometimes the road is long. The treasure deep within us must be nurtured and cared for, but once that treasure is discovered, we can go after it.

The amazing thing is that God has called us to be part of that sanctification process, to be part of removing skeletons and uncovering treasures, both in ourselves and in others. Galatians 6:2–3 instructs us, *"Brothers, if anyone is caught in any transgression, you who are spiritual should restore him in a spirit of gentleness....Bear one another's burdens, and so fulfill the law of Christ."* When we bear one another's burdens, we are helping to remove skeletons. When we restore another in gentleness, we help to reveal treasure. We have the great privilege of being part of this process for our kids. Know your children, knowing them is how you will know what and where their treasure is. You also need to know your children's skeletons, even—and perhaps especially—the ones you put there. Walk with them and help them uncover their treasures, their glory stories, the gifts God has given them—and then help them learn to use them.

UNPOPULAR PROMISES, BEAUTIFUL TRUTHS

Not every child is going to be a world-class athlete (or mathlete). Most are not going to be brain surgeons or CEOs or world-renowned authors. Every single child, however, is going to face hurdles, trials, and tribulations, and then each one will go on to face the same thing we all will face someday: death.

God has given us many promises in His Word, promises that are guaranteed. We love the promises of God in Scripture, but there are two promises that aren't very popular. Number one is the promise that we are going to struggle in this life, and number two is the reminder that someday we are going to die.

Read that again: We are going to struggle, and we are going to die. These are hard pills to swallow, but Jesus told us these truths to comfort us, not to scare us: *"In the world you will have tribulation. But take heart; I have overcome the world"* (John 16:33, emphasis added). Struggles and death are unavoidable, but Christ has overcome! We need not fear the trials.

WE ARE GOING TO STRUGGLE, AND WE ARE
GOING TO DIE. THESE ARE HARD PILLS TO
SWALLOW, BUT JESUS TOLD US THESE TRUTHS TO
COMFORT US, NOT TO SCARE US.

God has given each of us gifts, treasures uniquely designed to help us serve one another. Unfortunately, those treasures are often buried beneath skeletons, in danger of never being discovered or utilized. If we can bring out those hidden treasures—if we can minimize the pile of skeletons, cut down on the layers of bones between the treasure and the surface, where it can shine—then we can help our kids. We can minimize the things that hurt them—the things that push them down, make them depressed, and give them anxiety—and we can set them on a path to enjoying the treasures He has placed in them. *Christ in us can overcome.*

Anxiety, depression, oppression, ADD, ADHD, learning disabilities—everything has a pill that can be prescribed for it. They say, "Don't let your kids get hurt, don't let them fall, don't let them fail. Don't let them do this, don't let them do that." We need to understand that it's OK to watch them do things that might cause them to get hurt. They may get new scars, but they will become stronger. Sometimes we may have to let them experience hurt because, in the long run, the treasure will be greater; it will be worth more.

We greatly bless the young people in our lives simply by helping them unearth their treasures. In this way we get to partner in this "overcoming process," as Christ renews them day by day. If we can help young people find their God-given treasures as early as possible, then we help open a world of opportunity and understanding for them about how and why God made them and what their life's purpose may be. When they learn how to help others and how to give of their gifts, then a process begins whereby their treasures can rise through the bones and come to life on the surface. These young people can then flourish as the image bearers of God that He created them to be. They can be overcomers in Christ.

NINE

THE UNKNOWING ENABLER

I know a young man who can remember his first taste of alcohol as vividly as the clearing in the woods where it happened. He was twelve or thirteen years old, and he had just shot his first deer. He was with his dad, who told him, "First deer, first beer, as long as it's at camp."

At first glance, this sounds like an innocuous enough tradition. The father wanted his son to imbibe his first drink in his presence and in a controlled environment. The father had a chance to bond with his son by celebrating victory with a masculine activity, and the young man wouldn't be at risk of climbing into a car and driving.

The father, however, in an attempt to be friendly with his son, became an unknowing enabler. *Merriam-Webster* defines *enabler* as "one who enables another to persist in self-destructive behavior (such as substance abuse) by providing excuses or by making it possible to avoid the consequences of such behavior."[11] The enabler, in the recovery world, is often perceived as a key reason kids go bad. Enablers may allow young kids to drink and to be in situations where they experience feelings of euphoria when they are not yet mature enough to handle those feelings in safe and healthy ways.

---

11. *Merriam-Webster.com Dictionary*, s.v. "enabler," accessed December 26, 2023, https://www.merriam-webster.com/dictionary/enabler.

Often, enablers use excuses for kids' negative behaviors, saying such things as, "They'll grow out of it," or "It's just a phase."

The problem with enablers is that while they should be nurturing and caring for the young people in their lives, they are instead permitting and even encouraging poor choices. A child is going to suffer physically, spiritually, and emotionally from the problems brought on by substance abuse at a young age. Not everyone who has a beer as a teenager is going to end up with an alcohol problem, but for some, one choice can grow into a bad habit that quickly snowballs into full-blown addiction.

> NOT EVERYONE WHO HAS A BEER AS A
> TEENAGER IS GOING TO END UP WITH AN
> ALCOHOL PROBLEM, BUT FOR SOME, ONE CHOICE
> CAN GROW INTO A BAD HABIT THAT QUICKLY
> SNOWBALLS INTO FULL-BLOWN ADDICTION.

AVOID BEING AN ENABLING PARENT

Parents who act as enablers often have good hearts and love their kids unconditionally, they just aren't good at helping their children make smart decisions. In my case, my dad was too busy with his own life of addiction to notice that I was developing a problem or even that I was drinking at all, and he carelessly allowed me access to substances that should have been kept far out of my reach.

Young people tend to gravitate toward enablers, but what enablers don't realize is that this is manipulation. These young people are slowly and subtly destroyed as their parents, grandparents, or other guardians allow them to do whatever they want. This scheme is from the pits of hell. God's Word tells us that "*the thief comes only to steal and kill and destroy*" (John 10:10). Instead of stopping this destructive scheme instead in its tracks, enablers help it along.

GROWING ONE WAY OR ANOTHER

I often tell parents that we can't stop our children from growing. Whether we like it or not, they will grow—physically, emotionally, intellectually, and spiritually. The question is not *if* they will grow but rather *how* they will grow. Will they grow in the right direction or the wrong direction? As adults, it is our job to help our children grow in the right direction. Will we *equip* our children with the tools they need to withstand the attacks of the enemy, or will we *enable* them with destructive habits?

WILL WE *EQUIP* OUR CHILDREN WITH THE TOOLS THEY NEED TO WITHSTAND THE ATTACKS OF THE ENEMY, OR WILL WE *ENABLE* THEM WITH DESTRUCTIVE HABITS?

Helping our kids grow in the right direction isn't easy. The devil will dangle endless carrots in the faces of our children, and substance abuse is only one of them. Our kids will be tempted to date the wrong people, experiment with premarital sex, or make fun of the person everyone else is mocking. They may be tempted to cheat on tests, lie to those in authority, or begin dieting excessively to the point of struggling with an eating disorder. Fighting against these temptations is not for the faint of heart. In fact, resisting them requires tremendous self-confidence and faith, and it demands that children have parents committed to encouraging good choices along the way.

As parents, how are we directing our children? Do we know who their friends are and what they do to pass the time? Are they hanging with kids who work hard at school, enjoy appropriate recreational activities, and try to serve their heavenly Father? Or are they wasting their days with bored, directionless young people who would do anything for a laugh? If our kids are learning from the wrong kinds of peers, are there other groups or individuals we can steer them toward? Is there a youth group or Bible study in your neighborhood they could join? Even if you must drive to the next town so that your child can join a thriving, Bible-saturated, Christian organization filled with other young people committed to Jesus, the commute is going to be well worth it.

There are also other activities we can encourage our children to do that, while not necessarily Christian, will build their character and help them become the healthy, productive men and women God has designed them to be. Philippians 4:8 instructs us, *"Whatever is true, whatever is honorable, whatever is just, whatever is pure, whatever is lovely, whatever is commendable, if there is any excellence, if there is anything worthy of praise, think about these things."* There are plenty of activities out there that fall in line with the calling of this verse—activities that will teach our children how to be kind, how to think on those things that are "lovely" (such as art, music, or God's creation), and how to radiate light to those around them while pursuing endeavors that are commendable and excellent. Are you enabling your kids to be those kinds of young people in how they spend their time?

WAYS TO SUPPORT YOUR CHILDREN
WITHOUT ENABLING THEM

You don't need to be a wealthy parent to support your children's participation in God-honoring activities. For example, outdoor play can improve children's physical health, foster social interaction, and help them explore nature. It also allows them to get sunlight, which is wonderful for their bodies and brains.

Children who play outdoors will have freedom to do things that they can't do indoors, like race up a hill, climb a tree, or swing on a tire swing. If they're playing with friends, they'll learn about things like conflict resolution and making up fair games with rules. Kids can play at the basketball court, fish at the pond, or ride bikes around the block—the options are endless. They should *not* be "just chilling" in someone's basement all the time. It's not good for them. Boredom causes a lot of children to try things they wouldn't have considered if they had been engaged in other, positive activities.

Responsible parents will know where their children are and who they are playing with. Invite your children's friends over for dinner and get to know them. Do they seem trustworthy, kind, and respectful? Do they care about academics and extracurricular activities? You can also talk to the parents of your kids' friends to get an idea of the kinds of values being taught at home. Some parents are too strict, and others are too lenient. You should be navigating your child toward those friends who seem to be growing up in well-balanced homes.

In addition to intentionally encouraging healthy free-time activities with good friends, you can support your children by helping them pursue their skills and giftings, as we've discussed already. Your children may demonstrate talent for singing, acting, or running the bases. Do what you can to get them what they need to excel. This may require some sacrifice on your part to pay for lessons, register them for drama club, or sign them up for a team, but the sacrifices will be worth it as your kids spend time developing valuable skills and learning teamwork, self-confidence, and discipline. Even if your children don't end up performing or playing ball past high school or college, they will have spent their time building character rather than exploring unhealthy alternatives.

PROMOTE "FAILING FORWARD"

By participating in a wide range of activities, children find out what they enjoy—and they also find out that they don't have a knack for everything. There will be times when they fail, and other times when they realize they may not be cut out for certain activities. These are all good, healthy lessons.

In his book *Failing Forward*, John Maxwell talks about the missteps we all take and how we can use the lessons they teach us as stepping stones toward building more productive futures.[12] As parents, we can teach our children not to waste time beating themselves up for their shortcomings, for the areas in which they don't quite excel. Instead, we can ask them, "What lessons did you learn from this experience?" Maxwell argues that the difference between those who succeed and those who get lost in life is their attitude toward failure.

When you can learn from your failure and pick yourself up, allowing your Savior to help you, there's a wonderful future ahead of you. God's Word confirms this truth:

> *Count it all joy, my brothers, when you meet trials of various kinds, for you know that the testing of your faith produces steadfastness. And let steadfastness have its full effect, that you may be perfect and complete, lacking in nothing.*
> (James 1:2–4)

Long before anyone wrote books about the value of failing, Scripture told us that trials—which include our failures!—would complete us. Through trials we develop perseverance and steadfastness. Many successful individuals can identify a low point in their lives when they recognized their frailty and looked to God for answers. Teach your children not to let their mistakes go to waste.

TEACH YOUR CHILDREN NOT TO LET THEIR MISTAKES GO TO WASTE.

---

12. John C. Maxwell, *Failing Forward: Turning Mistakes into Stepping Stones for Success* (n.p.: HarperCollins Leadership, 2000).

None of us is without failure, and God knew we would all fall in profound ways. In fact, the Bible tells us in no uncertain terms, *"All have sinned and fall short of the glory of God"* (Romans 3:23). We need to let kids know that it's OK to make mistakes and follow them up with a course correction. We can do this without condoning the sin that's ensnaring them. Many young people can have a stronger future with the right kind of encouragement.

WHEN KIDS SAY, "IT'S MY CHOICE!"

As parents, my wife and I did everything we could to equip our children to grow in the right direction. We made it possible for them to do extracurricular activities. We let them fish and hunt. We took them to see the ocean. We gave them all the tools they needed to stand against the crafty schemes of hell, and yet, at one point or another, both looked us in the eye and said, "It's my choice." My daughter was so bold as to say, "Dad, you have given me every tool and have showed me how to avoid every negative thing, but I choose to do otherwise."

I had equipped both my kids to succeed, to make good decisions, and yet, like most young people, they preferred to make their own choices. When you're young, you think you're invincible and that you have the world all figured out. We were the same at that age! No one whose life seems to be going smoothly expects negative consequences. Young people often take for granted the current state of their life, thinking things will never change.

We need to keep in mind what God says about those who are called to nurture and care for young people. It is the job of parents and guardians to edify, stir up, and bring out the truth of God's Word in our young people—to equip them for a life of good things. There are many ways we can do this. When your children are younger, get them into God-honoring habits like going to church, doing devotions before bedtime, and praying before meals. As your children grow, you can provide them with age-appropriate

Christian books and bring them into situations where they will meet Christian role models who can motivate and inspire them.

CONSIDER THE EXAMPLE YOU SET

As adults, we need to realize that our kids are watching us more than they are listening to us. Are you talking to your children about the importance of Christian fellowship but neglecting to take them to church? Are you speaking highly about the virtues of marriage while mistreating your spouse? These are admittedly difficult things to face, but wise parents will look honestly at their lives and turn them around before making permanent, negative impressions on their children.

The traditional, stereotypical enabler who encourages bad behavior only wants to satisfy and give, trying to prevent any pain in a child's life. Enablers might do this for any number of reasons, including unjustified pain in their own childhoods. An appropriate amount of pain, however, should not be avoided at all costs, for it can lead to positive growth. This pain might include consequences for disobedience and poor decisions. In some cases, parents may need to enforce these consequences to help their children avoid even more painful repercussions in the future.

ESTABLISH HEALTHY, REASONABLE RULES

In my program we talk about a "refrigerator contract" (which I'll discuss in even more detail in the final chapter). This contract helps to curtail bad behavior and stop it in its tracks. We encourage moms and dads not to waste their time yelling and screaming but instead to write down what will happen if their children adhere to the family rules and what will happen if they don't. The first time you catch your underaged child drinking a beer, for instance, you write out the contract; the contract might say that if he uses alcohol again, he will lose screen privileges and nights out for a certain amount of time. On the other hand, if he makes good choices, there will be rewards. Both of you can sign that contract and stop bad behavior in its tracks. Be proactive; don't enable bad choices by ignoring them and pretending they will go away on their own.

It is important to understand an interesting nuance here with the contract. Notice that Mom and Dad aren't telling their kids, "You're bad," when they mess up, nor are they saying, "You're good," when they behave. Instead, once that contract is signed, it is between them and the contract. All you're doing as a parent is enforcing the contract, implementing the consequences if the contract is broken. In this way, the rules and consequences are upheld, but you're not in a fight with your kids.

With the contract method, your kids are not trying to earn your approval, only the rewards of right behavior. They are not trying to avoid your disapproval and disappointment, only the consequences of their behavior. This is important because we *all* need to learn that our actions have nothing to do with earning someone else's approval, not even God's.

IT ISN'T ABOUT EARNING

The wonderful news of the gospel is that God sent His Son to die on the cross *because He loves us*, not because we earned it. Romans 5:8 says, *"But God shows his love for us in that while we were still sinners, Christ died for us."* Likewise, Ephesians 2:4–9 says:

> But God, being rich in mercy, because of the great love with which he loved us, even when we were dead in our trespasses, made us alive together with Christ—by grace you have been saved—and raised us up with him and seated us with him in the heavenly places in Christ Jesus, so that in the coming ages he might show the immeasurable riches of his grace in kindness toward us in Christ Jesus. For by grace you have been saved through faith. And this is not your own doing; it is the gift of God, not a result of works, so that no one may boast.

THE WONDERFUL NEWS OF THE GOSPEL IS THAT GOD SENT HIS SON TO DIE ON THE CROSS *BECAUSE HE LOVES US*, NOT BECAUSE WE EARNED IT.

He accepts you. He has made you clean and worthy by Christ's sacrifice, not because of anything you have done to earn it but because of His great mercy and love. We should treat our kids the same way God treats us, offering them unconditional love and acceptance. This is why, with the refrigerator contract I just explained, we say that it's not personal. As parents, we tell our children that we love them, and that if they have any issues, it's with the rules, not with us. The rules are put in place because they are the natural outcome of living in a world of consequences. We reap what we sow in this life. The contract we make with our kids needs to be a microcosm, a reflection, of that reality. And there is ample room for unconditional love within it.

Children will grow through life's heartaches, but not if we make everything easy for them. I want you to know that children will not simply grow out of drug and alcohol abuse. We have to be intentional about equipping them to escape the snares of addiction and instead thrive in the good things of life.

I love Proverbs 22:6: *"Train up a child in the way he should go; even when he is old he will not depart from it."* In our family, getting our kids to church was just something we did. Our kids came to church with us because they are our kids. They went wherever we went, and they would come to church with us in the same way that they would accompany us to the beach or to a diner. There is more, however. We ought to be *training* them, like this verse in Proverbs tells us. We need to be preparing their hearts to grasp and receive God's Word.

We need to show our kids how to seek the Father when they face their first big hurdles. Ask them what God wants them to do and how they can grow in those challenges. There are lessons to be learned from broken hearts, and those lessons can teach our children to cling to Jesus and to commit themselves to doing what is right. We can also train our children to be thankful for the good gifts God has given them, including pillows for our heads at night, food on the table at mealtimes, and opportunities to soak in God's wonderful creation. Don't waste these opportunities to turn crises into profound moments for positive heart change.

THERE ARE LESSONS TO BE LEARNED FROM BROKEN HEARTS, AND THOSE LESSONS CAN TEACH OUR CHILDREN TO CLING TO JESUS AND TO COMMIT THEMSELVES TO DOING WHAT IS RIGHT.

SUPPORT GOOD DECISIONS

The poor choices young people make will eventually wear out a bad enabler, and the more tired the enabler is, the easier it becomes for the child to continue down the wrong path. A wise parent I know once told me, "You've got to make your big decisions on your best days." How true this is. The rough days are coming, and the rough days are not the days to be making hard decisions. Instead, think ahead. When everything is going great in the family, that is the time to make the big decisions and the tough calls. Those are the times to draw up the refrigerator contract and establish consequences. This way, when things get hard, you will only have to follow through and implement those decisions instead of wasting precious brain energy on debating and decision-making.

BE A "GOOD ENABLER"

I don't believe in tough love; I believe in unconditional love. We need to teach children to accept their choices, including their consequences, and then help them make better decisions. God gave each of us a conscience, the ability to know right from wrong. Our kids know when they've picked the wrong path. We need to be *"good enablers,"* helping our precious children admit when they have failed and then pointing them to the Father who makes all things possible.

WE NEED TO BE *"GOOD ENABLERS,"* HELPING OUR PRECIOUS CHILDREN ADMIT WHEN THEY HAVE FAILED AND THEN POINTING THEM TO THE FATHER WHO MAKES ALL THINGS POSSIBLE.

TAP INTO THE POWER OF PRAISE AND COLLABORATIVE DECISION-MAKING

When it comes to helping a young person make smart decisions, good old-fashioned praise goes a long way. Your child may have made some poor choices—deep down, your child knows that—but when your son or daughter makes a decision that pleases you, as well as their heavenly Father, show them that you notice and that you are proud! Don't add conditions or "you should haves" to your praise. Just let your young people know that you're thrilled they're living up to their potential.

You might also collaborate with your child to create a list of pros and cons when they are facing a decision. Pros and cons lists are great tools for helping children think through decisions logically. Start with simple choices, like what will happen if they eat only doughnuts for breakfast. On the pro side, you could list that they will love their breakfast and not complain about the first meal of the day. On the con side, you might write that they will end up exhausted when their sugar crashes in the late morning, and that in the long run they might put on weight and ultimately feel less motivated and confident. Then ask which healthier alternatives they could choose, and write these down together.

Continue by helping your children think through some more serious choices they might have to make. What would be the pros of drinking that beer, and what are some possible poor repercussions? Is the high or the "cool factor" worth the cost of the potential negative outcomes? If they are considering dating someone, you could ask: What are the person's positive attributes? What are their drawbacks? Are there steps that can help keep the relationship healthy and God-honoring? Are there individuals they can call when they're tempted to act inappropriately?

If you want children who choose well, make sure you surround them with others who see the best in them. Youth pastors, camp counselors, and godly friends and family members are the kinds of mentors that can inspire them and nurture their gifts. These men and women can reinforce the values you are trying to instill at home while modeling good decision-making skills that your children will want to emulate.

Remember, we have important jobs as *enablers for good* in our children's lives. We can enable healthy growth by encouraging our children's natural interests as they grow. God has designed us all with special gifts that we can use for His glory, and once your child is on the right path, there is no looking back.

TEN

GROUNDHOG DAY

At our group meeting every Thursday night, we had a regular visitor who was a young alcoholic. He didn't have a good home life. Each week he would come by for the meeting, dinner, and gym time, which he loved. He was super quiet. One night we were having a conversation with the whole group. I can't remember the topic, but he stopped me while I was speaking.

"Do you mind if I say something?" he asked.

I looked up, surprised. "No, go ahead," I said.

"Do you know what my life is like? It's like that stupid Groundhog Day movie," he began (only he didn't use the word *stupid*). "Every day I get up and crawl out of my hole. And I look around to the left and to the right, always wondering if someone is going to bother me or do something negative to me. At the end of the day, I crawl back into my hole. And I feel deep, dark, and hopeless."

I couldn't believe what I was hearing. You could have heard a pin drop on the carpet. As I looked around the room, I saw about twelve young people nodding their heads. Without saying a word, they were each telling me, "Yes, that's my life, also."

How dark must life be for these young people? They get out of bed every day, looking around for someone to show them how to live. A father is supposed to be instilling in them the truth that God's mercies are new every morning. A father should be showing these kids that joy is a choice they can make. Instead, these kids are fatherless. They don't know how to find light in a dark world, how to look for the positive things in life. They just wonder who's going to hurt them next, or manipulate them, or want something from them. They don't realize that there are second chances—that there is hope on the other side of the dark tunnel.

ONE DAY AT A TIME

As Christians we know that we can renew our minds each day with God's Word. His grace is new every time we wake up. That means that however we might have messed up yesterday, God gives us another opportunity today. We can thank God for His blessings, and we can lean on Him for hope. We can have faith that our heavenly Father will help us stay on the right path and empower us to make good choices. Those precious hours in the morning are critical for setting the course for the rest of the day, but without fathers showing these truths to young people, their lives can quickly become deep, dark holes.

As Christian leaders we can seek to fill these voids in fatherless hearts. We can engage young people in positive activities and pour into their lives the truths of God's Word. At the same time, too much truth at once can drown the plant. The "one day at a time" principle is good for everyone, not just for young people in recovery. It's important that we refrain from forcing our wills on others and instead rather care for and nurture young people, a little at a time.

TOO MUCH TRUTH AT ONCE CAN DROWN THE
PLANT. THE "ONE DAY AT A TIME" PRINCIPLE IS
GOOD FOR EVERYONE.

We also must understand where young people are coming from before we seek to nurture them. We need to understand the nature of the holes they are coming out of. Why is it so dark and deep for this person? Why does he have such a negative outlook on life? Is she being abused? Or did she experience a great scare as a child? Is this person's home simply an unkempt, depressing place with no one else around for company?

Once that young man shared his pain with us, we could begin caring for him on a different level. We knew we had to begin exposing him to the light, little by little. We would talk to this young man each week, and as time passed, he began exposing his fears in dribs and drabs.

"My hole is so dark and deep that I don't sleep a lot," he told me at one point. "I want to get out during the day to do something, but it's hard to get out. Yet underneath all of it is a sliver of hope. I don't know where it's coming from, but I'm always hoping and expecting that something will be different."

GET INTO THE LIGHT

Even groundhogs need to get out in the sun a little each day to go about their business. They spend most of their time burrowing, but even they get out into the light a little each day for food and water. In the same way, I believe that everyone seeks the light.

A person might get a job or volunteer somewhere or take a walk every morning. No matter what it is, there are plenty of options when it comes to activities to do in the light once someone has caught a glimpse of it. There are things people will want to do once they have felt that small sliver of hope. Their bodies begin to look to the light for vitamins and for life-sustaining power.

If we stay in the sun too long at once, we can get sunburned, but if we're exposed to it little by little, we get a base tan that provides protection. We can begin seeking what is good without being hurt by it.

GRADUAL PROGRESS

In recovery, the "one day at a time" principle is about waking up to the process and committing yourself anew each morning. You need to decide that you will remain sober for the next twenty-four hours, as this is a smaller, more achievable goal than committing to lifelong sobriety, and it will lead to your overall empowerment and success.

This principle is at play for us as we seek to renew the lives of young people. We can't expect a new outlook on life right away from those who have been struggling with addiction or depression. We can't expect the cure to be a new haircut, a good job, or a fun church outing. There must be a continual investment in the renewing of their minds. This may require some real listening and patience on our part, or even helping young people discover gifts, talents, and hopes for the future, as well as creating a solid plan for getting there. We won't be able to meet every one of their needs, but the Lord will show us how we can help, and we can do this with great joy, knowing that we are answering His call on our lives.

In our case, this young man saw a bit of light when he came to our group. He saw men acting like fathers, seeking to nurture young people and instill biblical principles in them. It was just a little bit of light, but it was enough to make him want more. He knew there was a better way of life possible, one where former addicts could become something positive and set an example for others. He still wasn't ready to receive it, but he could see that mercy, grace, and forgiveness were available to him. He saw that sliver of hope.

LEADERS LISTEN

As leaders it is our job first of all to just listen. There are many reasons why kids turn to addiction. They may have experienced childhood trauma; they may have become socially isolated due to bullying. They may be getting verbally abused and feel there is no hope for someone as flawed as they are. Whatever their situation is, it's important not to push truth and hopes on these young people too quickly. When they realize we are simply interested in who they are, then they will begin opening up, and this is where the Spirit of God can begin doing His work.

I would often ask this young man, "How long does it take you to get up and move in the morning? What are you looking for and hoping for this day?"

"Hopefully I will just get through the day," he would often respond.

Sometimes the best thing we can do as Christians is just be present and help others "get through the day." We can show young people a light that will make them wonder if more hope is possible. We can play ball with them, open up the Word to them, and offer them good food. We can talk to them about their problems, their hopes, and their dreams, all the while being examples of a father who genuinely cares about them.

SOMETIMES THE BEST THING WE CAN DO AS CHRISTIANS IS JUST BE PRESENT AND HELP OTHERS "GET THROUGH THE DAY."

The Bible tells us that "*the steadfast love of the* LORD *never ceases; his mercies never come to an end; they are new every morning; great is your faithfulness*" (Lamentations 3:22–23). Our heavenly Father knows our stories. He knows where we have been hurt, and He sees our potential. He knows where we have messed up, and

He continues to give us grace. We can show young people that God cares about who they are and about what their future can be. Our failures do not drive God away; He will never give up on us. Instead He keeps showing us how to take one step at a time, one day at a time. Young people can hear and understand these truths more and more when they realize just how loved and forgiven they are.

As adults in their lives, we can water them a little each day as they grow toward the sun. The light we shine must be so attractive that it points them heavenward. We must show them how grace and peace permeate our lives, making us hopeful, making us responsible. We can demonstrate how positive pursuits have overcome our addiction to the darkness and how we are now full of joy, consumed by the good works we do every day. First, however, we must listen. It always begins with listening.

DOING OUR PART

If you know someone struggling with addiction and you wish to be a light for that person, it's important to manage your expectations for the recovery process. You need to know, for example, that the behaviors and patterns associated with addiction probably won't change right away. There may be relapses, and it's important not to allow those things to deeply discourage either yourself or the recovering addict. Recovery is an ongoing process that requires lots of patience and mercy.

Those who are recovering also need a lot of joy that comes from healthy activities. Ask your loved one to accompany you on walks or to help you prepare meals. Spend this time talking about the mundane things of life, and avoid discussing addiction unless the person recovering brings it up. If possible, encourage the individual to join you in hobbies that are soothing, things like photography, crafting, or volunteering with animals. These activities are repetitive and life-affirming, nurturing a creative side without too much effort while also bringing your friend or loved one into a caring community.

DON'T NEGLECT SELF-CARE

If you're in the position of helping someone who struggles with addiction, it can be helpful for *you* to connect with other caregivers in the same position as you. The feelings you're having aren't as unusual as you may think. Find a well-established support group where others can help you see that you're not alone. This can help you stay strong psychologically, which is something you'll need as you try to support a recovering addict.

Self-care is important, and you'll want to make sure that you're eating, sleeping, and exercising if you're trying to be strong for someone else. Most of all, it's important not to take their struggles on yourself. They may need you to help and encourage them. You might even go to counseling alongside them. Keep in mind, however, that you are still your own person with your own thoughts, emotions, and plans. Keeping a healthy level of space is critical to maintaining your emotional well-being during a difficult time.

**KEEPING A HEALTHY LEVEL OF SPACE IS
CRITICAL TO MAINTAINING YOUR EMOTIONAL
WELL-BEING DURING A DIFFICULT TIME.**

Many of us will struggle when we are caregivers because we are supposedly the ones who are OK. In a similar situation, a man I know was caring for his wife as she battled cancer. At one point in their journey, they attended a conference focused on her particular type of cancer. There were large group sessions throughout the day that they could attend along with choices for various breakout sessions. One of the breakout sessions the man attended was for caregivers. He went in thinking it was going to be a workshop on how to provide better care for his wife, but instead it was all about how to take care of himself as the caregiver. Right away he felt a bit guilty attending this session, and he could see that others in the session felt the same. After all, he wasn't the one with cancer; his wife was the one who needed help and care.

It can seem selfish to worry about yourself when you're not the one with "the problem," but taking on another's struggle, whether an illness or an addiction, takes a toll, especially when you're caring for someone you love. You *must* take care of yourself. If you crash, you won't be able to help anybody, yourself included.

At the same time, you don't want to make the person you're trying to help feel like a burden. Our loved ones should know we genuinely enjoy their company. Do the best you can to listen in a nonjudgmental way. If you live with the person you're helping, try to establish good habits and a healthy routine. Keep rooms well lit, as this can help enhance feelings of well-being. Remind the person of how fulfilling life can be when we do the work it requires.

Today's world is full of young people who are swelling with pain and desperately need someone to listen. Even if the individual you're mentoring doesn't struggle with addiction, you can continue to be the light he sees every time he leaves the groundhog hole. Be positive, make jokes, and let him know he is still loved. A little bit of hope and care can go a long way. You could be the solid rock that someone has always known they needed to stand on so they could make a fresh start.

FINDING THE LIGHT

Many people watch the media coverage as a famous ground-hog named Phil emerges from his den every February 2 in Punxsutawney, Pennsylvania. Thousands travel there for the gath-ering each year—which includes a banquet, a talent show, and musical performances—and thousands more watch at home on television. Folks enjoy dancing and shopping while they're waiting for the groundhog to make his appearance, and it's quite a festive event. Depending on whether the groundhog sees his shadow and retreats to his den or not, there might be six more weeks of winter left, or an early spring might be on its way.

Some of us continue to live in these dark holes, just like that groundhog does all winter long. We might come out to get something to eat, but we always end up back in that hole. As soon as we start to emerge, the devil reminds us of why we were there in the first place as he seeks to *"steal and kill and destroy"* (John 10:10) any progress we've made.

"You don't have adequate financial resources," he whispers, or "You don't come from a good enough family." He continues to pile on the lies, making us doubt our skills and dredging up past mistakes we're ashamed of. This puts us in a negative place mentally, and the enemy tries to stake his claim.

The Lord wants us to continue coming out of that hole, however, and to begin living life to the fullest. The thief came to steal and destroy, but Jesus *"came that [we] may have life and have it abundantly"* (John 10:10). We can help people learn how to live productively. We can show others how to overcome. It's very easy to get overwhelmed by the darkness. If we spend enough time in a deep, dark hole, that space can start to seem dangerously comfortable. We begin blinking and fearing as we step into the light. But we must always push forward and help others do the same; it's our job to not retreat but instead keep walking toward the light.

I wish I could tell you that the young man we were helping found a happy ending to his story. The last I heard, he was living in the same area, still looking for the light in a bar. He goes to work to make some change yet continues to seek hope in a bottle of alcohol. Although I can't say he is walking with the Lord or that his light shines as brightly as it can, I do believe a seed of hope was planted deep within him. I am trusting the Lord that it will be watered, nurtured, and cared for, and I am praying that one day he will emerge from his hole and begin walking in the true light of the presence of the almighty God.

ELEVEN

ONE WRONG TURN

Before the time of cell phones and GPS apps, taking a wrong turn was more of a predicament than it is today. You'd be jetting off to a party or dashing out for a road trip, and suddenly it was no time to celebrate. When you realized you were lost, a worn map would be anxiously yanked from your glove compartment as you tried to figure out where you were and which steps you had to take to get on the right path. If you were traveling at night, it was hard not to panic as you peered out over the landscape of empty streets and closed convenience stores. Once you finally returned to the intersection where you'd made the error, a feeling of relief would wash over you like a cold shower on a scorching summer day. You knew where you were again, and you could resume your journey.

Most young people will make wrong turns as they edge out onto the road of life, but they often find themselves without GPS, or even a paper map, as they feverishly scan the roads around them for any type of directional indications. Street signs and mile markers would let them know their location and how they could begin retracing their steps, but these aren't so easy to find out there in the dark. Once they've taken a wrong turn or two, finding their way back will cost precious time and energy, or they may continue heading down a series of dead-end streets, blindly hoping one of them will lead them to something familiar.

LIFE AT THE CROSSROADS

Even children who grow up in the healthiest, most supportive homes need to understand there are crossroads coming in their lives. For now, they may have their parents making decisions for them, including where they should go to church or what they should wear to school, but there will come a time when they are going to have to make these calls on their own—and they won't always make the right ones. They may choose friends who mistreat them or romantic partners who hurt them. They may make a fool of themselves after drinking too much.

EVEN CHILDREN WHO GROW UP IN THE HEALTHIEST, MOST SUPPORTIVE HOMES NEED TO UNDERSTAND THERE ARE CROSSROADS COMING IN THEIR LIVES.

Satan loves to use these times to create chaos in the lives of young people in the form of chain reactions. Young adults may make poor decisions, and the enemy will begin telling them they are no good and capable only of ruining their opportunities. Such mindsets are incredibly discouraging and can lead these tender souls to seek refuge in alcohol or illicit relationships. Such downward spirals of self-loathing and negative behaviors can go on for the long term if left unchecked.

NOT ALL THOSE WHO WANDER...

There's a famous line of poetry in J. R. R. Tolkien's *The Fellowship of the Ring* that reads, "Not all those who wander are lost."[13] It is important for young people to understand that one bad decision does not equate to a wasted life. Young people can learn

---

13. J. R. R. Tolkien, *The Fellowship of the Ring: Being the First Part of The Lord of the Rings* (New York: Ballantine Books, 1965), 231. Citation is to Seventeenth Printing, 1990.

to dust themselves off and move forward with faith and determination. This is why it is so critical that they understand their self-worth. If you build up children when they are young, they will have healthy attitudes toward the mistakes they will inevitably make. They will begin exploring and learning lessons from their mistakes, knowing that it's OK to admit their mistakes and course correct. For children who aren't secure in who they are, however, wrong turns can be devastating as they begin to see those wrong turns as evidence of their inadequacy.

Often, youths are tempted to take wrong turns because they think the right path won't produce the things they want in life. They may have had negative upbringings where they were taught that the traditional road is unloving, unkind, and full of darkness. Young people who have had positive feedback, however, will be more willing to stay on the right path and more determined to find their way back to it if they stray. They will understand that one failure does not define them. They are worthy and wiser, ready to retrace their steps, chalk up their mistakes as learning opportunities, and try again with gusto.

YOUNG PEOPLE WHO HAVE HAD POSITIVE FEEDBACK WILL BE MORE WILLING TO STAY ON THE RIGHT PATH AND MORE DETERMINED TO FIND THEIR WAY BACK TO IT IF THEY STRAY. THEY WILL UNDERSTAND THAT ONE FAILURE DOES NOT DEFINE THEM.

I've always said that you don't get apples from an orange tree, and cornfields won't grow from grass seed. A young person who comes from a positive, life-affirming home will be much more likely to withstand the inevitable disappointments of life. Jesus said, "*Out of the abundance of the heart the mouth speaks. The good person out of his good treasure brings forth good, and the evil person out of his evil treasure brings forth evil*" (Matthew 12:34–35). Whatever our children are hearing and seeing will go into their hearts; it will become what they treasure, and this will impact how they live. If they are constantly hearing negative things, it will be much harder for them to stay on—or return to—the narrow path. If they are strong in who they are in Christ, however—if we have helped them store up "*good treasure*" in their hearts—then life's ebbs and flows will be outmatched by their confidence in their heavenly Father.

BELIEVING IN OUR KIDS—AND LETTING THEM KNOW IT

What are we telling our children that will strengthen them? Are we showing them that godly parents believe in them, no matter what they do? Do we remind them daily that God has unique purposes for their lives? Are we showing and telling them that failure is not final and that God's love will prevail? Or, conversely, are our words and actions demonstrating that their mistakes make them unworthy? Could we be so busy trying to force our agendas on them that we don't realize how we're making them feel?

Know that being entrusted with the care of a young person is a huge responsibility. You are the source your child is looking to for strength, encouragement, and nurturing. You are the voice of inspiration that your son or daughter needs to hear in the groundhog hole. The world will have plenty of influences trying to pull your child down into darkness. Make sure you are always pointing your child to the light.

AVOIDING WRONG TURNS IN THE MIND

Sometimes even kids born into the most advantageous circumstances end up taking wrong turns, and these poor decisions can impact them physically. They might suffer injuries because of a reckless night or miss out on educational opportunities because they lacked self-discipline. Once they've made these kinds of wrong turns, it's usually easy to pinpoint where the error occurred and then steer them back to the right path.

A more insidious type of "wrong turn," however, is the type taken in the mind. People can get caught up in negative patterns of thinking that can hold them back their entire lives. For these folks, no matter what circumstance they find themselves in, they never seem to be victorious in their minds. An individual like this might move across the country, get a new spouse, make a fortune, or even break a Guinness World Record, yet still feel unhappy and lacking. Let's take a look at some of these negative thought patterns so we can learn how to avoid them and how to help our kids break them.

THE GUILT TRAP

One common example of negative thinking is being stuck in a rut of guilt because of something you did or said. No matter where you are or what else you're doing, the enemy will bring up reminders of your past in an effort to drag you down. You may feel like you shouldn't be enjoying your life or being productive because you have failed.

Our enemy thrives on making us think we are undeserving of God's love and that we've sinned too badly to be forgiven. When you are tempted to think this way, remind yourself that *"God shows his love for us in that while we were still sinners, Christ died for us"* (Romans 5:8). Your sin is not a surprise to God, and nothing you have done can separate you from His love.

YOUR SIN IS NOT A SURPRISE TO GOD, AND NOTHING YOU HAVE DONE CAN SEPARATE YOU FROM HIS LOVE.

SELF-CRITICISM

We may also be tempted to get caught in a web of negativity and self-criticism. Those who have been picked on in their youth may be particularly susceptible to this. For example, they may always tell themselves things like, "I can't do this; I'm going to fail." When they are in unfamiliar situations, they may be prone to panic attacks because they don't believe they can rise to the challenge.

However, God has called us to lives without fear, and we can be confident in our worth in the eyes of the Lord. When we are tempted to think negatively, we must remind ourselves of the promises of Scripture. For example, Romans 8:28 tells us that *"for those who love God all things work together for good, for those who are called according to his purpose."* Our Lord has equipped us with everything we need to live out the purpose He has designed us for, and even when we mess up, He can still use our mistakes to achieve His end.

CATASTROPHIZING

Another negative thought pattern is catastrophizing—jumping to the worst possible conclusions about a scenario. We may mess up on a small scale and then convince ourselves that we are useless, or we might have a small setback, like a late start to college, and begin telling ourselves that things are doomed to always be behind schedule. This can be quite the defeating mindset in a world where things rarely go exactly as planned. Healthy individuals learn to cope with minor setbacks and keep them in perspective.

DENYING WRONGDOING

Believe it or not, another negative thought pattern that holds young people back is the inability to admit they are wrong. Insisting they are right when they aren't isn't admirable, and this pattern can quickly become an unpleasant personality trait that keeps them stuck in their ways, unable to make the changes necessary to help them grow and become healthy contributors in the workplace and in their homes.

We're all familiar with John 3:16, which talks of God sending His only Son to save us because of His great love for us. But not everybody is familiar with what Jesus says just a few verses after that:

> *And this is the judgment: the light has come into the world, and people loved the darkness rather than the light because their works were evil. For everyone who does wicked things hates the light and does not come to the light, lest his works should be exposed. But whoever does what is true comes to the light, so that it may be clearly seen that his works have been carried out in God.* (John 3:19–21)

Coming into the light means facing the truth and being honest about our own sins and shortcomings. No one likes to admit when they are wrong, but doing so will yield great rewards. We need to let our children know that it's OK to make mistakes and admit that they need to do something differently. Learning to admit mistakes is key to maturing into healthy adults, and since we're all human, this is a skill our kids will likely have to repeat many times in the future—and a skill that we as adults should be practicing regularly, as well!

Getting out from under the spells of these negative ways of thinking may be more difficult for some people than for others. Speaking to a Christian counselor may be necessary to help some young people break free from these self-defeating streaks. We must remind our kids that there is always a way back if they are willing to turn to God in faith. Wrong turns of the mind will continue to impact relationships, professional goals, and emotional health until a person is willing to surrender to God. The good news is that it's never too late to make the right turn back in His direction, and He will always meet you where you are.

DISCERNING DIFFERENT PERSONALITIES

As a grandparent now helping to raise my grandson, I must admit that the ways I see him, treat him, and nurture him are different from the way I treated my own kids as they were growing up. This is because time and experience have taught me some lessons that have led to wisdom. It is also often easier for grandparents to accept the positives and negatives in children's temperaments that parents sometimes don't want to see. They are therefore often better equipped to discern unique personalities in kids and to nurture them accordingly.

THE CHOLERIC CHILD

Certain children, for example, have choleric personalities. These kids are outspoken and competitive, determined to win. We used to call kids with this type of personality "strong-willed."

Persistence is one of those traits you've got to admire in choleric youngsters. They know what they want and aren't easily deterred by setbacks. They can be a real handful to raise, however. When they don't get what they want, they may go so far as to scream or physically protest (kicking, hitting, biting) to get you to go along with them. Firm boundaries, a calm tone of voice, and a sense of humor are required for these children. You will need to let them know you recognize their strengths and that you continue to believe in them. Often, choleric children can become quite successful because they are undeterred by opposition from others.

THE SANGUINE CHILD

At first blush, children with sanguine personalities might seem easier to raise. These young people are playful, sociable, and enthusiastic. You'll probably find them riding bikes around the block with their friends or putting on plays in the living room. These children aren't afraid of risks and often have an adventurous spirit.

Their fun-loving hearts, however, often make them impulsive and averse to discipline. They may see rules as restrictive and cruel because they want to be free to have a good time. Parents of sanguine kids have the unique challenge of establishing clear expectations and enforcing accountability without damaging a child's free spirit and sense of self. Creative outlets, such as music and art, can often help them to achieve this balance.

THE MELANCHOLY CHILD

Children with melancholic personalities are deep thinkers. You may often catch them reading books or journaling. They thrive on tradition and order, keeping their rooms clean and completing their homework on time. If you have a melancholic child, you likely have little to worry about when it comes to teaching them to be disciplined and tidy.

These types, however, may also be quiet and moody, strongly preferring solitude over socialization. Melancholic children will require as much praise as any others. They may also need you to remain cheerful and relaxed, showing that you can be a steady force in their world of emotional roller coasters. Such children may also require an extra push to get them out the door for baseball games or playdates. Allow them to spend time with peers that seem to accept and understand them, even if they would rather spend most of their time alone. All children need at least some healthy interaction with others their own age if they are going to develop properly. Know that your child's ups and downs are natural to their personality, and don't try to change them. Instead recognize their gifts and affirm them as often as possible.

THE PHLEGMATIC CHILD

Finally, those with a phlegmatic personality type are generally very warm, trusting, and considerate. They may be cuddly and are often eager to help their friends and family, and often you'll find them curled up with a good book in their favorite chair. Phlegmatic children can sometimes be difficult to motivate as they prefer to stay in their comfort zones and out of the spotlight. It's easy for them to go along with the flow and not make waves, but it is important to constantly affirm their gifts and encourage them to develop them, even if that means stretching them a bit. This may make them uncomfortable, but you'll want to give them plenty of chances for success so they can learn how to thrive in a world full of driven individuals.

Great caregivers will respect the special strengths and weaknesses of each child, no matter the personality type. They will learn when to be firm and when to tread more lightly in those times when criticism might be devastating. They will figure out how to motivate their children without destroying their spirits. The finest caregivers know how to adapt their parenting style to suit the needs and strengths of the child they have been entrusted with nurturing. Ask God for wisdom, and He will provide you with all the insight you need.

TURNING BACK TO THE RIGHT PATH

In my own life I have witnessed both my son and my daughter take wrong turns in their late teens, which came with dramatic consequences. I have also witnessed God take those moments and use them to shape my kids into the fine adults they are today.

One reason kids are prone to getting lost after they take wrong turns is that they don't believe they can turn back and embrace life anew. They know it will be more difficult to get back to the right path once they have strayed from it, and they fear that process of returning. We must remind them that *"he who is in you is greater than he who is in the world"* (1 John 4:4). It is possible for young people to be brought back to God after they have made one, five, or even ten wrong turns. We must help them understand the potential dangers of veering from the right path while also encouraging them to overcome their inevitable mistakes. We must teach them that God has not given up on them, and neither will we.

IT IS POSSIBLE FOR YOUNG PEOPLE TO BE
BROUGHT BACK TO GOD AFTER THEY HAVE
MADE ONE, FIVE, OR EVEN TEN WRONG TURNS.

TWELVE

AT ARM'S LENGTH

When a parent child-proofs a house, he or she considers the types of dangers their kid could get into—those things at arm's length that could endanger their child's well-being. What are some of the things at arm's length for today's kids? When I use that phrase, you might picture a cell phone or a remote control. Young people can pick these items up easily and instantly be entertained.

The problem is that objects at arm's length can also provide youngsters with opportunities to make bad choices. Teens can pick up their devices and spend hours shopping or looking at degrading images of people, or they might go on social media and notice that their friends are hanging out without them. Even if what they're looking at isn't necessarily hurtful or sinful, they could be ignoring individuals who want to spend time with them while they head down the Internet rabbit hole. These are precious years and relationships that they won't be able to reclaim later on.

What every child *should* be experiencing at arm's length are such things as hugs, love, and approval from their parents or guardians. Many children, however, will never experience such signs of affection. Instead they might get hit or constantly face the look of disgust or disappointment in their parents' eyes.

Most young people will also find themselves within arm's length of their first opportunity to try drugs or alcohol. They can choose to say no, or they can choose to give in to peer pressure. It's easy for children to make poor choices when they're given too many options, but if young people are properly nurtured and cared for, they can make good choices and learn how to overcome even their bad decisions.

SOWING AND REAPING

Many believers today operate under a type of "holy wishful thinking." They succumb to unrealistic expectations, both for themselves and for their children, thinking that they will become instantly wealthy or that their children will turn out perfect, simply because that's what they desire.

The Bible warns us, *"Do not be deceived: God is not mocked, for whatever one sows, that will he also reap. For the one who sows to his own flesh will from the flesh reap corruption, but the one who sows to the Spirit will from the Spirit reap eternal life"* (Galatians 6:7–8). We should not be surprised when our poor decisions—choices that are contrary to the Word of God—yield a harvest of lack and disappointment. We should let our children know that this is to be expected in their lives, as well. They cannot carry on lives of substance abuse, sexual permissiveness, and laziness and then expect happy, abundant results. The Bible tells us that this abundant harvest comes only if we sow to the Spirit.

WE SHOULD NOT BE SURPRISED WHEN OUR POOR DECISIONS—CHOICES THAT ARE CONTRARY TO THE WORD OF GOD—YIELD A HARVEST OF LACK AND DISAPPOINTMENT.

How do we "sow to the Spirit"? A simple beginning is to follow the Ten Commandments as well as the principles outlined in all of Scripture. Young people should aim to be honest and hardworking at school and in their social lives. They should try to keep their thoughts and actions pure. Forgiving others, demonstrating kindness, and listening to and bearing the burdens of friends are also things God will honor.

We can also teach sowing in terms of finances. Children as young as seven or eight years old can be taught to put away some of their money each month and to give a certain percentage to the Lord. Children who learn to save and tithe will see God's hand working in their bank accounts when they are grown.

PATIENT PURSUIT

We must understand that the rewards folks are hoping to see may not come right away. In today's world of prosperity preaching, we often expect to be promoted or to inherit a windfall the minute we decide to turn around and do things God's way. The Bible tells us that blessings are not always immediate but come to those who persevere: *"And let us not grow weary of doing good, for in due season we will reap, if we do not give up"* (Galatians 6:9). Children and adults alike must be taught to be patient, trusting that they will see the fruits of their labor in due time.

CHILDREN AND ADULTS ALIKE MUST BE TAUGHT
TO BE PATIENT, TRUSTING THAT THEY WILL SEE
THE FRUITS OF THEIR LABOR IN DUE TIME.

And what are the rewards of faithfulness? The Bible tells us about the fruit of the Spirit—love, joy, peace, patience, kindness, goodness, faithfulness, gentleness, and self-control. (See Galatians 5:22–23.) Imagine living your life with an abundance of peace and joy! Each day you get up and do the best you can without struggling with feelings of guilt and inadequacy. Instead you are confident, knowing that you are doing what is right in the eyes of your heavenly Father and that God will provide meaningful ways for your life to be a glowing beam of hope in a world mired in hurt and shame.

Choosing the narrow path is difficult for young people, just as it is for anyone. They will struggle with peer pressure and with the desire to do whatever pleases them. The care and love of a single committed adult, however, can make all the difference. How are you helping your young person through struggles and temptations? Are you encouraging your loved one to pray about these problems? Are you helping your son or daughter find good work that will keep Satan from gaining a foothold? Or are you reacting harshly and consequently encouraging secrecy and deception?

Remember that our kids are learning from what they see in us much more than from what they hear us say. Are they watching us overreact to worldly problems and underestimate the power of God? Do they witness parents who seek solace in bottles of beer or secret affairs? Or do they see us down on our knees, searching for answers that only God can provide? Are we showing them how to be faithful even when it's difficult, or are we just talking about it?

Sometimes it's challenging for parents to admit when they fail, since their lives serve as witnesses to the next generation, but we must know that even in the worst of circumstances, there is forgiveness. God is willing to restore us and begin using our lives for good, no matter where we are or what we have done. In time we will reap that harvest of righteousness if we do not give up.

LET THEM PUT OUT THEIR OWN FIRES

I am always fascinated by new technology and how it can benefit us. Growing up, we didn't have GPS to tell us how to get somewhere. We just had to trust the map or the person who gave us directions. Today our phones can show us exactly where we are, map out the most direct route to our destination, and even indicate the roads that will take us through the least amount of traffic.

Thanks to artificial intelligence, a kid today can even get in a car with no driver and end up at the right destination! Technology can be great in a way. For those children who have been experiencing trouble with drugs and alcohol, self-driving cars offer a way to avoid worrying about them driving drunk and hurting themselves or someone else. At the same time, this can become a crutch that encourages them to drink or get high because some of the potential consequences of those decisions are eliminated.

The same idea is at play when we think about how we used to pull our kids' hands away from stovetops when they were young. At a certain age it is appropriate for a parent to constantly monitor the child, because a little one might feel that the stove is hot before touching it and reach for the burner anyway. At some point, however, children must learn that when they feel the heat, they shouldn't touch the stove. And it is at that juncture—at that place of comprehension—that children must learn how to take ownership of their decisions and put out their own fires.

Children won't learn if we are always rescuing them from the repercussions of their actions. At some point we need to let them feel the heat. If they abuse drugs and alcohol, they might end up ruining their school performance or their friendships. It's important that, as parents, we resist making excuses for them or blaming someone else for their actions. Instead, we should talk frankly with them about how their own behaviors have contributed to their state of disappointment. We can encourage them to try again, doing it God's way this time. We can also let them know that peace and hope are waiting for them on the other side of their good choices.

CHILDREN WON'T LEARN IF WE ARE ALWAYS
RESCUING THEM FROM THE REPERCUSSIONS OF
THEIR ACTIONS. AT SOME POINT WE NEED TO
LET THEM FEEL THE HEAT.

When we teach kids to walk, we keep them safely at arm's length. We let them toddle toward us, knowing they will probably fall but that we will be there to help them up. As parents, it can be difficult to put our children down on the carpet and let them try walking on their own. We are sometimes tempted to just keep carrying them forever! Our children will never learn how to make their way in the world, however, if they don't figure out how to get around without someone else carrying them.

In the same way, it is important for us to allow our children to experience the consequences of their actions while we wait for them at arm's length. We can show them empathy and teach them the lessons that mistakes bring, but we should also be teaching them how to walk, how to live life with purpose and integrity. At arm's length, we become the quiet source of guidance that our kids desperately need.

A SAVIOR AT ARM'S LENGTH

Whenever we need something that's out of reach, we naturally reach for a chair or stand on our tiptoes. Our arms sometimes aren't long enough, and we know we've got to reach out for help. Are we teaching our kids now, while we have them at home, how to reach out? Are we teaching them Whom to reach out to?

ARE WE TEACHING OUR KIDS NOW, WHILE WE
HAVE THEM AT HOME, HOW TO REACH OUT? ARE
WE TEACHING THEM WHOM TO REACH OUT TO?

When we send our kids off to college or to work or to the military, we know we can no longer always be there for them, telling them to stay away from that bottle of beer or that inappropriate relationship. Even if we are still geographically close to our children, we can't tell them which career to choose or when to start a family of their own. They grow up and start making decisions on their own, as they should, and it's impossible for us to force our kids to make good financial choices or to save for the future. All we can do is teach them the right things while they are in our homes and hope they will be wise in decision-making when they get older.

As our kids grow up, they too will begin to understand that we are not always there. At the same time they will also realize that they can't get through life on their own. They need help! Even adults long for a parent who will love them, nurture them, and support them as they make difficult decisions and try to follow their dreams. We need to point our kids to their heavenly Father—the only Parent who can provide them with all the unconditional love they need, wherever they are, throughout the rest of their lives.

Jesus died on the cross with outstretched arms for our children. He will guide them, nurture them, and wrap His arms around them. When your children need support, He can provide a church family that will pray for them and provide good advice. When they make poor decisions, He can show them forgiveness and gently direct them forward. He can care for all their needs, even when we aren't there.

How are we showing our children a loving Savior while they're still in our homes, a heavenly Father who will never leave or forsake them? Are we demonstrating how to seek counsel through the Bible, prayer, and wise Christian mentors? Are we displaying forgiveness when they fail? Are we doing everything we can to make the gospel attractive to them?

I'm sure none of us has done this as perfectly or as completely as we could have, but we must allow our Savior to forgive us, and then we must begin modeling true faithfulness for our children. As they grow, they will become lights to a world in desperate need of hope.

GROWING UP

The physical process of growing is natural and predictable as kids get older. They get taller and develop adultlike bodies. If we provide proper nutrition and exercise, they should be growing out of sizes and needing gradually larger clothes until they are in their teens or twenties. It seems that we parents are always filling up the fridge with food and filling up closets with shoes and shirts that fit! We understand that physical growth is a natural part of life, and we don't question these changes.

In the same way, our children are always growing spiritually. As I've said, they may be growing in positive ways or in negative ways, but they are always growing. Our enemy continually looks for ways to discourage them or cause them to become angry and bitter so that they will get stuck. He wants to start the destructive cycle of frustration, addiction, and self-hatred. We parents need to do everything we can to create positive trajectories for our children's spiritual growth instead.

While taking your children to church is important, you'll also want to model at home what it means to be part of God's family. After morning worship, discuss the sermon on the drive home, or ask your kids what they learned in Sunday school. When kids are little, they may enjoy hearing Bible stories at night, sometimes asking for favorite narratives to be reread. As they get older you may want to help them pick out age-appropriate devotionals and Christian fiction with characters who are the same age and gender as they are. This is a great way to keep kids entertained while reinforcing your family values. You can also give them biographies of well-known Christians for inspiration. Encourage your kids to set aside time every night before bed to read the Scriptures and pray, and model this behavior yourself.

Many parents choose to take their kids to Christian camps or retreats where they can enjoy lots of hands-on activities, like swimming and ropes courses, with a Christ-centered perspective. Values such as kindness, honesty, and self-control are reinforced while everyone has a great time. Kids learn Christian songs and develop friendships with other believers their age, and they can see young adults modeling positive Christian decisions that they can then emulate as they begin to mature.

Some parents also institute family nights where individuals play board games, enjoy meals together, and have meaningful devotional times. There are also many faith-based movies you could watch and discuss. If children are unsure of their faith and have questions, it's important not to turn away those questions or make children feel ashamed. Instead, use these family times to provide safe outlets for asking questions and exploring answers together. We want our young people to have a solid foundation as they move out into the world. While the home isn't the only place where they can get this, we can do our best as parents to make sure they see this modeled under our roofs.

**WE WANT OUR YOUNG PEOPLE TO HAVE
A SOLID FOUNDATION AS THEY MOVE
OUT INTO THE WORLD.**

There's a well-known proverb that says, "Give a man a fish and you feed him for a day; teach a man to fish and you feed him for a lifetime." When we teach kids how to fish, we instruct them in how to sustain themselves when they are hungry. They learn how to touch a hook without getting hurt, as well as how to bait it and how to cast the line.

As parents we eventually have to stop "catching fish" for our kids. When they are old enough, they will know they need to leave the shore to get fed, and they will have the tools, the skills, and the understanding to make that happen. They will understand they must go fishing at the right time of day if they are to get enough food for themselves and for their families. Most important, they will know how to call on the great Fisherman whenever they are stuck, knowing He is always right at arm's length.

THIRTEEN

CONVICTION VERSUS GUILT

None of us likes feeling guilt. In fact, holding on to it long-term can cause a number of emotional and even physical problems, including depression, insomnia, and social withdrawal. Guilt has a terrible connotation today and recalls images of people consumed by feelings of shame and regret, unable to function properly, mired in ugly emotions that keep them from enjoying life.

As Christians, we know those feelings are sometimes a call to action, alerting us to something that needs our attention. We have done wrong, and we need to seek forgiveness. Many times, however, we continue to beat ourselves up even after we have sought forgiveness, and that is never of God. We need to recognize the difference between conviction, which comes from the Holy Spirit, and guilt, which comes from Satan.

GODLY GRIEF

Many of us know the overwhelming feelings of anguish that can take over our lives when we have done something wrong and haven't confessed to it. When the truth comes out, we suddenly feel a tremendous sense of relief. Whatever the repercussions are, the truth has come out. We are freed from the burden of being the only one who knows what happened, and we can begin making amends. As John 8:32 says, *"The truth will set you free."*

The Bible talks a good bit about these "bad feelings" we experience when we have sinned. For instance, 2 Corinthians 7:10 says that *"godly grief produces a repentance that leads to salvation without regret, whereas worldly grief produces death."* What exactly is *"godly grief"*? Godly grief is that feeling of sadness that comes over us when we realize we have hurt others as well as God. It is a deep realization of the damage our words or actions have caused. As this verse teaches us, godly grief eventually leads us to repentance, which means we express sincere remorse and turn around. We seek forgiveness from those we have offended, as well as from God, and we seek to change our actions moving forward.

GODLY GRIEF EVENTUALLY LEADS US TO REPENTANCE, WHICH MEANS WE EXPRESS SINCERE REMORSE AND TURN AROUND.

For example, imagine your child stole money from you and then blamed his brother or sister. He might feel good about it for a while, thinking he got away with something, but then guilt starts to set in. He begins to see how his sibling is suffering, and eventually he is no longer able to shoulder these feelings of guilt. He confesses the truth to you (including his sibling's innocence), accepts the consequences of his action, and returns the cash. He vows never to steal again and demonstrates his commitment to this by getting a part-time job where he can earn his own money and thus reduce the temptation to take what doesn't belong to him ever again.

When our grief is godly, we seek forgiveness from our heavenly Father. We admit we have done wrong, and we trust that He is loving enough to absolve us of our negative feelings. We can then move on with our lives, stronger for the lessons we have learned and committed to avoiding this type of offense for the rest of our lives.

Conviction is another word for godly grief. The dictionary defines *conviction* as "the act of convincing a person of error or of compelling the admission of a truth."[14] When we feel convicted, we are driven to admit that we are in the wrong. There is no more hiding it, and we are disingenuous if we try. Instead we openly admit what we have done, while also acknowledging the depth of sin in our hearts, and we find a forgiveness that allows us to move on.

One classic biblical example of godly grief, or conviction, is that of Peter. He denied Jesus publicly three times after his Savior had been arrested, just as the Lord had predicted he would (see Luke 22:54–62). When Peter saw Jesus looking at him, he knew what he had done wrong, and Scripture tells us that *"he went out and wept bitterly"* (verse 62). This was not the only time Peter messed up. Peter is also the disciple who tried walking on water with Jesus but took his eyes off the Lord and began to sink (see Matthew 14:28–30). He also attacked the servant of the high priest when Jesus was being arrested (see John 18:10).

This is not the end of Peter's story, however. In fact, Peter became the rock, or foundation, upon which Jesus said He would build His church (see Matthew 16:18–19). In the book of Acts we see Peter was the main speaker on the day of Pentecost (see Acts 2). Peter played a pivotal role in the writing of the gospels, as well, since the gospel of Mark, written by John Mark, was based on firsthand accounts that Mark heard from Peter. The apostle also wrote the two epistles that bear his name. Peter certainly sinned big—but that wasn't the end of his story. God turned Peter's godly grief, his conviction and repentance, into beautiful things for the kingdom.

As Christian leaders it's important for us to be honest about our kids. They will make mistakes, and some of those mistakes,

14. *Merriam-Webster.com Dictionary*, s.v. "conviction," accessed December 26, 2023, https://www.merriam-webster.com/dictionary/conviction.

just like Peter's, might be big. Peter wept because he knew he had grieved Jesus, but he never became so overwhelmed by his sin to the point of giving up. Peter sinned big, but God's grace in Christ is always bigger. Peter is proof that God can mightily use those who are willing to ask for forgiveness and that He lovingly guides those who turn to Him in their sin. We need to demonstrate this to the next generation, no matter how difficult it might sometimes be.

PETER SINNED BIG, BUT GOD'S GRACE IN CHRIST IS ALWAYS BIGGER.

WORLDLY GUILT

In contrast to the *"godly grief"* described in 2 Corinthians 7:10, there's another kind of grief, and this kind of grief doesn't do us—or anyone else—any good: *"Godly grief produces a repentance that leads to salvation without regret, whereas **worldly grief produces death"** (emphasis added). Worldly grief is the sad, sorry state of guilt that we often mistake as a proper response to our sin. This guilt results from embarrassment or fear. We are simply ashamed of what we have done, but instead of taking steps to confess, seek forgiveness, and make it right, we wallow in our feelings of guilt. Then we keep feeling bad about how bad we feel. It's a vicious cycle, and it often leads to even more sin as we search for a quick fix to our pain.

An example of worldly sorrow in the Bible is Judas Iscariot, the great betrayer who turned Jesus over to the chief priests in exchange for thirty silver coins (see Matthew 26:14–16). Judas was later overcome with remorse for his betrayal of the innocent Jesus. The priests washed their hands of their part in the act, saying the responsibility lay squarely on the former disciple's shoulders. Judas's sense of worldly guilt was too great for him, and he took his own life to escape that crushing sense of guilt. He did not have a sense that God could ever forgive him, so he allowed himself to be consumed with self-hatred, taking his own life because he believed it was the only way to end his misery. Instead of confessing and seeking forgiveness—which would have brought relief and life— Judas threw the thirty coins at the temple and went out to hang himself (see Matthew 27:3–5).

As Christians we are often shocked by the story of Judas, yet how often do we succumb to the same sort of thinking? How often are we consumed by guilt and shame instead of looking to Christ and the forgiveness we have in Him? When we sin, are we tempted simply to ruminate on our regret, hoping we can feel bad enough to atone for what we have done? Do we seek comfort in substances, pornography, or picking on those we feel to be even more sinful than us? Do we refuse to be forgiven by God, continuing to carry a weight of sadness because we believe that is the only thing we deserve?

**DO WE REFUSE TO BE FORGIVEN BY GOD,
CONTINUING TO CARRY A WEIGHT OF SADNESS
BECAUSE WE BELIEVE THAT IS THE
ONLY THING WE DESERVE?**

The only healthy solution in these moments is to place our trust in Jesus. Most Christians are familiar with the verse that says, *"For all have sinned and fall short of the glory of God"* (Romans 3:23). Each of us has sinned in ways that make us unacceptable to a holy God. The next verse, however, reminds us that all *"are justified by his grace as a gift, through the redemption that is in Christ Jesus"* (Romans 3:24). That is wonderful news! No matter who we are or what we have done, God can still redeem us through the person and work of Jesus Christ. Our job is only to accept the gift and stop trying to save ourselves through guilt and sadness.

IS IT WORLDLY GUILT OR GODLY CONVICTION?

We want to turn away from worldly guilt and instead nurture godly conviction, and the first step to doing that is being able to differentiate between the two in our own lives. What are the signs of worldly guilt, and what are the signs of godly conviction?

When we feel worldly sorrow, we aren't troubled that we have offended God and His holiness; instead, we are just embarrassed by how the sin makes us look to others, and we are upset about the consequences we are suffering. You know you are lost in worldly sorrow when you spend days feeling sorry for yourself. You relive the moments in your head and think about what others must be saying about you. You are overwhelmed with shame and know that you can't forgive yourself in your current state.

By contrast, godly conviction won't stick around long. It is in your heart and soul long enough to make you turn to Jesus and then ask forgiveness from those you have hurt. While godly sorrow may cause temporary pain, we are grateful for it in the end because it leads us to change. We begin being more careful with our words and avoiding gossip. We start working harder and spending less time idling away. We no longer have alcohol in our homes and avoid it altogether, seeking to fill our days in community with other believers instead, working for the kingdom.

WHILE GODLY SORROW MAY CAUSE TEMPORARY PAIN, WE ARE GRATEFUL FOR IT IN THE END BECAUSE IT LEADS US TO CHANGE.

Those who have experienced godly conviction become passionate about salvation, which they know is the only true hope they have. They want to see justice done for those they have wronged. They discover a newfound distaste for sin, including all the worst parts of themselves that sin brings to the surface. Most profound of all, they no longer feel regret. Those who have experienced godly sorrow don't beat themselves up or relive embarrassing moments with no end in sight. Instead they believe they are absolved of their shame, thanks to the work of their Savior, who is enough.

This is why Jesus instructs us not to worry (see Matthew 6:25–34). We cannot add time to our lives or nice things to our wardrobes just by fretting about it. In the same way we cannot fix ourselves through constant grief or earn forgiveness through perpetual regret. These things are fruitless wastes of time. When our children do wrong, they won't be able to climb back up on the horse of life if they are trying to guilt themselves into positive living. Instead we must show them how to go to their Savior with their sorrow. Only He can forgive them and show them how to do better.

ENCOURAGING GODLY CONVICTION

Unfortunately, many Christian parents today set poor examples for their children of what conviction should look like. They discipline their kids by talking about the shame they are bringing on the family name, or they make fun of them so they feel even deeper embarrassment. This will do little to bring young people into a right relationship with their Savior, into a place of godly conviction and repentance.

Sometimes we see our kids expressing worldly sorrow and recognize it for what it is. They might whine and express self-pity, look for comfort by blaming others, or say they couldn't help what they did because of an unfair situation they were placed in. Kids experiencing worldly guilt will also feel tremendously bad about the consequences of their actions instead of feeling sorrow for the action itself. We may see them trying to bargain down their punishment, stomping and crying and pleading with us to change it, while never even acknowledging what they did wrong to produce the consequence.

If we want our children to demonstrate godly conviction rather than worldly guilt, we need to keep things uncomplicated. Deep down, everyone is aware they have done wrong when they sin. Tell your children that you love them, but that they have disappointed you and that their sin makes God, sad as well. Set an appropriate consequence for the action. This will change as kids get older. Instead of time-outs, they may lose driving privileges for a time. Older children may be sharper with their words and better able to hurt you when they are upset, but you will need to hold the line. You can also talk to them about the very real potential consequences of continuing in their sin. Drunk driving accidents with lifelong repercussions, STDs—these are real problems they could have to face if they continue on their current path.

It is important, however, to end your discipline on a positive note. Express your confidence that your child will be able to turn it around, and remind your son or daughter that God is pleased when we repent. You can reframe repentance as something that isn't shameful and remind them that we can be grateful that God always forgives. It is vital to model this type of attitude as adults. When we hurt someone or lose our cool, we can simply admit our mistake, ask for forgiveness, and move on. We don't need to spend our time talking about how tired we are or how no one helps us around the house, or wallowing in self-pity and false guilt. Instead, allow *yourself* to learn the lesson of godly conviction; it will bring freedom to your own heart and set a profound example for the young people watching you.

ALLOW *YOURSELF* TO LEARN THE LESSON OF GODLY CONVICTION; IT WILL BRING FREEDOM TO YOUR OWN HEART AND SET A PROFOUND EXAMPLE FOR THE YOUNG PEOPLE WATCHING YOU.

This is also not the time to overreact to our children's misbehavior. It can be tempting to yell and scream and tell our youngsters exactly what we think of them. We might feel shocked, humiliated, and ashamed, wondering what we did wrong as parents to cause our children to sin in this way. Resist the urge to think like this, as it will only lead to despair and unnecessary bad blood between yourself and your child.

Instead, plant your feet firmly and remind yourself that *you too are a sinner saved by grace*. Your child needs firm boundaries, mercy, and hope that can only be found in Jesus. Do your best to provide firm guidance and advice, but know that they might not be ready to accept it yet. Above all, remind them that the love of God, as well as your own approval, has not changed.

To nurture and guide young hearts is a serious task, and we should always approach it with a sense of gravity. In showing our kids the difference between worldly guilt and godly conviction, we help them more fully grasp the gospel, the good news that God's abundant mercy and grace is freely offered to them in Christ. God can do wonderful things with them, even though they haven't lived their lives perfectly. He can use their mistakes to make their stories robust and inspiring. When good kids go bad, the last thing we should do is give up. We should be ready and willing to help them take the next step.

FOURTEEN

A VISION FOR RECOVERY

I want to use this last chapter to talk about Young Overcomers United (YOU). As mentioned in the introduction, YOU is a non-profit organization that was conceived on October 1, 1995. Just as God was faithful in the beginning to work out the miraculous details that made this organization possible, He has been faithful through the years in using this ministry to rescue countless people from drug and alcohol abuse and, more important, to win souls to Jesus Christ.

Eventually I went to a local church and asked if we could meet there because our organization was getting too big for my house, which was certainly a good problem to have. They agreed, and we grew from around fifteen people to forty-five rather quickly. After that the Lord graciously allowed us to move into another facility. We call it "the warehouse"—a large building donated to us where we nurture and care for young people.

P3: PARENTS PRAYING FOR PARENTS

Another arm of YOU, for which we began to see a need, is called P3—Parents Praying for Parents. As we ministered to young people, we began to meet many of their parents, who loved them, cared for them, and were at the end of themselves when it came to knowing how to help them. Since the day we first asked these parents twenty-seven years ago what their number one need was, we've been getting the same answer: "Can you pray for us?"

SINCE THE DAY WE FIRST ASKED THESE PARENTS TWENTY-SEVEN YEARS AGO WHAT THEIR NUMBER ONE NEED WAS, WE'VE BEEN GETTING THE SAME ANSWER: "CAN YOU PRAY FOR US?"

Whether it was, "We've lost a child to drugs," or "We've lost a child to alcohol," or "We have other children in the house who need your prayer," the resounding cry was always the same—these parents needed prayer. Parents began to get together from all walks of life and all kinds of churches and just sit there together. As we sat, we realized our common bond: We were all hurting, because we had these same issues in the home. When someone loses a loved one to drugs or alcohol, it is very difficult to know how to start picking up the pieces. When someone in the house is addicted, it is hard to know where to turn.

We have some parents who have been there and have turned the corner, and their young person is now doing well. Sometimes, however, it is hard for them to be in the same room with other parents in the middle of it, parents with the same needs they once had. It is triggering and traumatic. The systems of P3 work well, though, because we are all like-minded. We all know what it is like trying to help someone with drug and alcohol abuse problems.

We try to nurture and care and come alongside, giving the tools that are needed. When someone asks how many people we have in the program, I like to remember that our goal is not to have *anyone* in the program. We provide the tools for people to get spiritually, physically, and even financially healthy and out on their own as quickly as they can.

The hardest thing at YOU is teaching people how to live again. When their lives have revolved around drugs and alcohol, this is a great challenge, because abusing drugs and alcohol is how people have learned to get through the day. They now need something new to live for, something else to center their lives around. They need to remember the things they loved before substances robbed them of so much.

Our goal is to hit all trigger points through teaching people, caring for them, and then training them for different areas of life. We try to help them identify their hobbies or interests as we find their uniqueness, their "fingerprints." Just as everybody has a set of fingerprints that is unique, we all have unique personalities, wirings, temperaments, and giftings. God has wired each of us uniquely, and no one has lived the exact same life as anyone else. There are patterns, but everyone's recovery is different.

INTERVENTIONS

We meet every Thursday night, except for Thanksgiving and Christmas (if Christmas falls on a Thursday). We do make ourselves available twenty-four seven, however, for home interventions. I've lost count of how many interventions we have done. We get a phone call and we go, like an EMT team summoned by a 9-1-1 call. Each one is different, and if even you've seen an intervention on TV, you haven't seen yet what we do, because there is nothing like it.

Before doing anything else, I mobilize the P3 parents, and they start storming heaven with intercession, ushering us spiritually into the situation and loading up our ultimate weapon against the addiction—a prayer-empowered presentation of the good news of Jesus Christ. After that, we go in and assess the family dynamics.

An in-home intervention begins with a phone call, usually from a crying parent who got our number from another parent who has been in the same situation. When I walk through the door, there is usually a group of people there. I look for the oldest grandma in the room, because, nine times out of ten, she has already been praying for the situation and has spiritual stability and the wisest perspective, having watched the young person raised from birth by his or her parents.

One thing we understand is that we are not there to intervene in the life of one kid; we are there to intervene in the lives of the whole family, because the young addicted person is not usually ready to listen to us and wants nothing to do with getting help. The young person doesn't want any spiritual intervention, and don't think for a minute that his or her resistance is not spiritually motivated. Remember that our struggle is not against flesh and blood but against the rulers and principalities of evil (see Ephesians 6:12 KJV). If we go into one of these situations without realizing it is spiritual warfare, we will lose. We are trying to take back what is rightfully God's in a life that's been turned over to the drug and alcohol world.

ONE THING WE UNDERSTAND IS THAT WE ARE NOT THERE TO INTERVENE IN THE LIFE OF ONE KID. WE ARE THERE TO INTERVENE IN THE LIVES OF THE WHOLE FAMILY.

After conferring with the elder prayer warrior, we start looking for fingerprints. Every person's recovery is different and comes with unique "prints" because of family dynamics. To help someone, we must understand these dynamics. Who's in it to win it? Who just wants it to be over? Who's saying, "I did it when I was young; they'll grow out of it"? (As an aside, that sentiment is never true. You only grow *into* addiction, not *out of* it, and the drugs available to young people today are more dangerous than those of their parents' day, with higher intensity and easier accessibility, making quitting that much harder.)

This initial process of "breaking down the door" and meeting the family takes about two to three hours. We break the ice and study the family members to identify key players. We assess the mom and dad, and we typically find that they are not on the same page. One is ready for change, desperate to get help, no matter the cost. The other is not taking the addiction seriously, and this is a major hurdle in the process. There is a young person making bad choices, but there is usually one enabler among the parents, helping that young person stay trapped.

I bring truth, I bring love, and I bring the heat. I have a brash personality that you are either going to love or hate, but you'll want to know what I have to say, because it is biblically based. I don't yell or scream. I don't tell people what to do. I don't park a van outside and say, "You're going to rehab!"

We nurture, care, and persuade, allowing parents time to wake up and start understanding the gravity of the situation. They start realizing they have some tough choices to make. This is why an intervention is not usually a one-night event; it's one night at the start of a very long road. I cannot tell you, though, how many miracles we've seen where God moves in the heart of recalcitrant family member, and the whole family begins a concerted effort in prayer. Through this, the young person begins to wake up to the severity of the problem and begins to desire help. We've witnessed this miracle multiple times—of a young person waking up, seeking help, getting saved, getting clean, and then ultimately getting *free*.

WE'VE WITNESSED THIS MIRACLE MULTIPLE TIMES—OF A YOUNG PERSON WAKING UP, SEEKING HELP, GETTING SAVED, GETTING CLEAN, AND THEN ULTIMATELY GETTING *FREE*.

BEING FREE

I will say once more that there is a huge difference between being clean and being free, and freedom does not come without a surrendered life to Jesus Christ. When I prepare to do an intervention, I go in with that attitude—I'm not going for *clean*, I'm going for *free*. I go in the back door with the gospel of Jesus Christ, and I come in as if I'm flying a 747 jet; it's quiet, and I'm going to land it.

If you're doing an intervention, you put on your boots and fasten your seat belt: you're in for a long ride, and the intervention is only the beginning. I know of people who want to be interventionists, and I don't know why. It's brutal work. The road to recovery has to start somewhere, though, just like the road to addiction started somewhere.

REFRIGERATOR CONTRACTS

Freedom from addiction doesn't come easily, and neither did our freedom from sin come easily for Christ. He paid a high price for it, and so will we if we start down that road. We teach and prepare the families, even when the young people don't want to hear what we have to say. We show families that if they are going to do the same things they've always done, they will get what they've always gotten. It's just common sense.

This is why we are big on refrigerator contracts, as I mentioned earlier. Once the parents get on board and understand there are going to be some incredibly tough decisions, we have everyone sign a contract. There will be days when everything is going haywire and tough decisions will have to be made. The days that are even harder are the good days, the easy days, the days when you can forget there is even a problem. On those days, families can look at that contract posted on the fridge and the commitment they made, remembering that they're not done.

The refrigerator contracts are made when everyone is focused and on the same page. We write them when there is clarity about the process so that later, when everything is unclear, we can go back to the time when we were thinking straight and follow the plan we established, step by step. This includes the understanding that, if you adhere to the simple rules of the contract, you can stay at YOU, and we will continue to pour out ourselves to help you at all costs. If you buck the system, however, and you want to go back to your own way, then you and your family are on your own.

THERE WILL BE DAYS WHEN EVERYTHING IS GOING HAYWIRE AND TOUGH DECISIONS WILL HAVE TO BE MADE. THE DAYS THAT ARE EVEN HARDER ARE THE GOOD DAYS, THE EASY DAYS, THE DAYS WHEN YOU CAN FORGET THERE IS EVEN A PROBLEM.

The language here is crucial and must be precise. We never "kick out" anyone, and we never recommend a family say they are "kicking out" their family member from the home, because that is not what is happening. What *is* happening is that the addict is choosing to remove himself or herself from the program and from the home. They are always welcome, but if they do not adhere to the contract, they are *removing themselves*. They are declining help.

THE PARENTS ARE CRUCIAL

For those who "fail," do you want to know where it usually breaks down? The parents. It is the parents who often don't have the courage to stick to the plan and follow through with the consequences. This is not hard to understand because we are asking them to break a pattern that has been set in since birth, a pattern of empty threats and promises.

These are often the parents who raised their children saying, "If you don't stop making that noise, we won't go to the pool"—but then still went to the pool even when their children did not obey. Sometimes these parents also made exaggerated threats, such as, "I'm going to kill you." How can we expect their kids to believe what their parents tell them? When kids grow up on a steady diet of empty or exaggerated threats, one thing is for sure: They will have difficulty understanding that actions have consequences. One of our biggest battles at YOU is very often with the parents, trying to get them to become *consistent*.

WHEN KIDS GROW UP ON A STEADY DIET OF EMPTY OR EXAGGERATED THREATS, ONE THING IS FOR SURE: THEY WILL HAVE DIFFICULTY UNDERSTANDING THAT ACTIONS HAVE CONSEQUENCES.

We have learned through the years what works and what doesn't work. If we sense that the parents aren't on board, then we abort the intervention, because we know it will never work. Those parents who are fed up and ready, however, have a very good chance of success with their addicted loved ones. Many times we go in at the stage of planting seeds of hope. Other times, we are watering those seeds. And at still other, wonderful times, we are harvesting freedom. Each story of recovery is different. One thing is certain, though: To see a family restored when a kid gets free is plenty fuel for the next hundred interventions. It is a wonderful and enormous blessing.

TEN STEPS

The intervention is just the beginning. After the intervention, the power of our assistance lies in the ten-step process to freedom that we've identified and upon which we base our program. These steps have been designed with the understanding that recovery is a spiritual battle.

Briefly, here is our list of ten steps. I will then go into detail on each one.

+ Step one: ACKNOWLEDGE that I have a problem or addiction.

+ Step two: MAKE a decision to be free from the things I'm involved with.

+ Step three: ACCEPT that I was made for a specific purpose and that God has a perfect plan for my life.

+ Step four: RECEIVE SALVATION (THE WAY TO HEAVEN).

+ Step five: GIVE GOD all authority and lordship over my life.

+ Step six: FORGIVE myself. God's will is that I forgive myself.

+ Step seven: BUILD A BRIDGE, asking for forgiveness from those I've wronged.

+ Step eight: BE CAUTIOUS! BACKSLIDING HAPPENS!

+ Step nine: COMMIT myself daily to Christ by reading His Word and praying to Him.

+ Step ten: FIND a home church and get involved.

STEP ONE:
ACKNOWLEDGE THAT I HAVE A PROBLEM OR ADDICTION.

It is so powerful to face the truth. So often we get caught up in addictions because we don't want to admit we have a problem. We look away from the mirror and ignore the truth about our hurts and the hurts we are causing others. We're ashamed, so we drink or do drugs even more to forget. But there must be a moment when we stop lying to ourselves. This is one of the most powerful actions we can take apart from simply surrendering to God. As the prodigal son *"came to himself"* (Luke 15:17), we must do the same, looking hard into the mirror and accepting the truth.

STEP TWO: MAKE A DECISION TO BE FREE FROM THE THINGS I'M INVOLVED WITH.

We can face the truth of our addictions, but then what? We have two real choices: life and death. We can decide to turn away and move toward freedom, or we can just keep drinking and dying until we're done and we stop breathing. Some say they can manage their addictions, but these folks don't truly want to be free. They are operating under the illusion that they can control their addictions, when the reality is that their addictions will control them. As we say in our program, there is a price to pay for freedom; it is sacrifice.

STEP THREE: ACCEPT THAT I WAS MADE FOR A SPECIFIC PURPOSE AND THAT GOD HAS A PERFECT PLAN FOR MY LIFE.

We need to accept that we were made for a purpose. *"For we are his workmanship, created in Christ Jesus for good works, which God prepared beforehand, that we should walk in them"* (Ephesians 2:10). Many people turn to drugs and alcohol because they simply do not know and understand that they are here for a God-ordained reason. The first step to discovering your purpose is to believe that you have one.

STEP FOUR: RECEIVE SALVATION (THE WAY TO HEAVEN).

We do not want to run off and try to achieve our purpose without the empowerment of the Holy Spirit, without the humble confidence that comes from accepting the free gift of sonship in Christ, the salvation that comes through faith alone, by grace alone, in Christ alone. Jesus Christ died for all who would believe in Him and in His sacrifice for us. He holds out a promise of love and acceptance to all who would be saved. The gift is eternal life and a new life in Christ. *"For the wages of sin is death, but the free gift of God is eternal life in Christ Jesus our Lord"* (Romans 6:23).

JESUS CHRIST DIED FOR ALL WHO WOULD
BELIEVE IN HIM AND IN HIS SACRIFICE FOR
US. HE HOLDS OUT A PROMISE OF LOVE AND
ACCEPTANCE TO ALL WHO WOULD BE SAVED.

STEP FIVE: GIVE GOD ALL AUTHORITY AND LORDSHIP OVER MY LIFE.

This step can be summarized in the question "Who is making my decisions?" If you have accepted salvation, the free gift of eternal life in Christ, then the next step is to offer yourself up to His lordship. He has put His perfect Holy Spirit inside you to lead, convict, and empower you toward the things to which He has called you. We must surrender daily to His will and base each decision on the truth of His Word, the Bible. *"The LORD will keep you from all evil; he will keep your life. The LORD will keep your going out and your coming in from this time forth and forevermore"* (Psalm 121:7–8).

STEP SIX: FORGIVE MYSELF. GOD'S WILL IS THAT I FORGIVE MYSELF.

God has forgiven you if you have trusted Him for salvation. Do you think He would not want you to forgive yourself? *"There is therefore now no condemnation for those who are in Christ Jesus"* (Romans 8:1). The sins and mistakes of your past occurred because you were either unregenerate or weak in faith. Allow the truth that God has *"cast all [your] sins into the depths of the sea"* (Micah 7:19) to set you free from guilt and shame for past deeds. You really are made new! Believe it, and forgive yourself.

STEP SEVEN: BUILD A BRIDGE, ASKING FOR FORGIVENESS FROM THOSE I'VE WRONGED.

Just as it is powerful to be honest with yourself, so too is it powerful to be honest with others. If you have broken trust with others, then it is especially crucial to confess to them and seek their forgiveness if you are going to live in the light. You will rebuild trust as people see that you are not the same person you used to be when you hurt them. *"Therefore, confess your sins to one another and pray for one another, that you may be healed"* (James 5:16).

STEP EIGHT: BE CAUTIOUS! BACKSLIDING HAPPENS!

Now that you have surrendered your life to Christ and are walking in His truth and His purposes for you, keep moving forward in His grace. Backsliding happens when we are not vigilant to abide in Him (see John 15:5). Sometimes this happens when we become overconfident and start living by our own strength rather than daily depending on Him and His power. Continue to seek help when you need it. God's plan for you is a long-term plan as long as you live. Never stop surrendering, and you will not backslide into old ways. Stop moving toward Him, however, and you will backslide. *"Cast your burden on the LORD, and he will sustain you; he will never permit the righteous to be moved"* (Psalm 55:22).

STEP NINE: COMMIT MYSELF DAILY TO CHRIST BY READING HIS WORD AND PRAYING TO HIM.

Jesus committed Himself and dedicated time every day to prayer, and we must do the same. It is dedication, rather than desire, that controls my destiny; prayer is the doorway that will guide my life. Additionally, time in the Word, the Bible, trains my mind and heart to know Him, to know what He wants, and it is a time of fellowshipping with Him. Each day we become more and more who we truly are by abiding in Him in prayer and in His Word. This is a part of surrender, and it is a true blessing to be called into the glorious presence of God in Christ.

IT IS DEDICATION, RATHER THAN DESIRE,
THAT CONTROLS MY DESTINY; PRAYER IS THE
DOORWAY THAT WILL GUIDE MY LIFE.

STEP TEN: FIND A HOME CHURCH AND GET INVOLVED.

The church was God's idea to support the believer and give him or her a spiritual family to belong to. The local church is an expression of the worldwide body of Christ across time. If there are other Christians around you, then being around God's people, spending time in worship, participating in discipleship, and taking part in shared missions are not optional. Ask the Lord to show you which functioning church He would have you join, and then go and share with them what God has done for you. *"As each has received a gift, use it to serve one another, as good stewards of God's varied grace"* (1 Peter 4:10).

Those are our ten steps—the steps that we encourage people in our program to do. We have seen again and again that they are powerful when followed. If you are reading this and need support following these steps, please contact us!

THE SAVED WHO DON'T GET FREE IN THIS LIFE

One amazing thing about our ten-step program is that even if someone is unable to get clean from addiction, if they go through the steps, their freedom is only delayed until they go on to be with Jesus.

Unfortunately, in the twenty-seven years we've been doing this, we have been to quite a few funerals. The saving grace for us is knowing that we have impacted these young people and that we have seen with our own eyes and heard with our own ears the dedication of young people who have accepted Christ as their Savior, trying daily to make Him the Lord of their lives. Having made one or two bad choices, they end up passing away through addiction or overdose. This is always heartbreaking, but we also know we can rejoice, for they are now in the presence of Jesus, no longer in bondage.

We know the most important thing young overcomers need for us to do is to plant seeds of hope. Every time we meet somebody, we plant a seed of hope. When we see him or her again, we water that seed and watch it come to fruition.

LEARNING TO LIVE AGAIN

One of the most practical things we do is teach young people how to live again. A couple times a year we will take young people on trips and spend lots of time with them. One of our favorite trips is a getaway where we teach young people how to fly-fish for steelhead and king salmon. We rent a house, and we have a sober weekend, or a sober five-day getaway, learning how to live again with no drugs and no alcohol. We start each morning early with devotions, surrendering our lives anew to Christ, and then we ask God to give us strength to get through the day, to learn to live again without drugs and alcohol, and to have an incredible day that will lead to a new lifestyle. Females who don't want to fish will go do different things. My wife takes them to different activities and nurtures and cares for them doing the things they love.

In this way, our approach is different. We don't give a keychain for a day sober or a week sober. There's nothing wrong with that, but we give them Bibles, we give them hoodie sweatshirts, we give trips to New York and Lake Erie, and we teach them what they need to learn so that they can live again.

Throughout the year we have one-on-one discipleship training classes and Christ-centered meetings. No matter what we're doing, though, we've learned to do it in a way that has young people starting the conversations. Young people have a desire to show us how they need to be nurtured, and they will prompt us in the right direction. We keep our ears open so we can better help them learn how to live life again.

What led to their addictions in the first place? Wasn't it a failure to live their lives? They had come to a point where they didn't know what to do with themselves. They were without purpose and without healthy outlets for dealing with the anxieties, fears, and insecurities of life. It is important that we provide some of those things, those healthy outlets, if they are going to stay clean.

Young Overcomers United is just an outreach supported by different churches, and we are on call twenty-four seven. YOU could be an outreach of every single church; I believe we could be plugged in at every single youth group. Drugs and alcohol come right out of the pit of hell, weapons of Satan to trap the minds of young people so that it's difficult to get out. But we know that through seeking the Lord and committing to Jesus Christ, a young person can walk in freedom, and at Young Overcomers United, we promote freedom.

Remember, there is a huge difference between being free and being clean. You can be clean and sober but still not be free. Once you know what God has done through His Son, however, you can start walking in freedom. It's amazing when young people have that desire to seek God through a simple prayer. We simply must nurture and care for them.

YOU CAN BE CLEAN AND SOBER BUT STILL NOT
BE FREE. ONCE YOU KNOW WHAT GOD HAS DONE
THROUGH HIS SON, HOWEVER, YOU CAN START
WALKING IN FREEDOM.

We have had multiple young people in our program who have been in for five, six, or seven rehabs, and some of whom have overdosed three or four times. These same young people, when they hear the good news, the gospel of Jesus Christ, say, "Why haven't I heard this before? Why haven't I been told that I can walk in freedom—freedom over the dominion of darkness?"

Our approach is unorthodox, but we do get the job done, and we never give up. We plant seeds of hope. Some people plant the seed, some people water the seed, some people harvest the fruit. We do a little bit of everything, but most of all, we accept young people for who they are and what they are, right where they are. Young Overcomers United is an ongoing ministry that helps young people, one person at a time. If you are in need of our services, or if we can help you begin a ministry in your church, please contact us.

ABOUT THE AUTHOR

Joe Maxim, aka Big Joe, grew up near Pittsburgh, Pennsylvania. The youngest of eight children, he struggled with addiction during his early teen years and into early adulthood. When he finally beat his ten-year addiction around the age of twenty-four, he chose to help others do the same by beginning Young Overcomers United (YOU). What started with just one young person in his home has since become a source of hope for hundreds of young addicts and their families looking to change. Since 1995, Joe and his wife, Chris, have given young people the tools they need to succeed in recovery. In many cases, Joe encourages them to become leaders themselves, helping others to achieve freedom from addiction. Creating change in the lives of tomorrow's leaders is his ultimate goal.